The Negotiation
of Cultural Identity

The Negotiation of Cultural Identity

Perceptions of European Americans and African Americans

Ronald L. Jackson II
Foreword by Molefi Kete Asante

Westport, Connecticut
London

Library of Congress Cataloging-in-Publication Data

Jackson, Ronald L., 1970–
   The negotiation of cultural identity : perceptions of European
Americans and African Americans / Ronald L. Jackson II ; foreword by
Molefi Kete Asante.
      p.   cm.
   Includes bibliographical references and index.
   ISBN 0–275–96184–2 (alk. paper)
   1. Group identity—United States.   2. Race awareness—United
States.   3. Afro-Americans—Race identity.   4. Social surveys—
United States.   I. Title.
HN57.J2464   1999
305.8′00973—dc21   97–50041

British Library Cataloguing in Publication Data is available.

Library of Congress Catalog Card Number: 97–50041
ISBN: 0–275–96184–2

First published in 1999

Praeger Publishers, 88 Post Road West, Westport, CT 06881
An imprint of Greenwood Publishing Group, Inc.
www.praeger.com

Printed in the United States of America

The paper used in this book complies with the
Permanent Paper Standard issued by the National
Information Standards Organization (Z39.48–1984).

10 9 8 7 6 5 4 3 2 1

This book is dedicated to, first and foremost, the one who goes by infinite names. The Lord Jesus Christ is the primary source of my strength and fortitude. All the glory and honor is due unto God.

To my lifelong inspirator, Sharon Marie Prather, my mother. She has encouraged me to pursue all of my goals and has been a true exemplar of perseverance. It is through her constant support and unflinching confidence in me that I have been perpetually motivated to complete this chapter in my life.

My father, Ronald L. Jackson, Sr., has also been ever vigilant by uplifting my spirits, accompanying me in my aspirations, and providing a listening ear. I have come to realize over the years that the unconditional love of my mother and father is unmatched. Saying thanks is only a morsel of gratitude I offer them at these momentous crossroads.

With my deepest love and appreciation, to my soulmate, best friend and spouse, Ricci, for her patience, love, encouragement, and tolerance during our most turbulent times.

In the spirit of the African tradition, praise is awarded to the deceased, the living, and those not yet born. During the completion of this book, my newest joy was borne, Niyah Simone Jackson. I dedicate this book to her with the hope that she will pursue her dreams relentlessly keeping God first always.

Contents

Figures and Tables

Foreword

Ronald Jackson has taken us to the depths of ourselves and has shown us how we consciously or unconsciously approach the negotiation of cultural spaces, whether interrogated or uninterrogated. What is at stake in the push toward postmodern onticity is the proper positioning of all the social and cultural identities that we possess, as either "black" or "white" interactants in an increasingly multicultural milieu. The danger is not that we will lose our identities but the possibility that our identities have already been lost in some places and spaces where we've been. Consequently, we are ourselves searching throughout this intricate web of antagonistic and oppositional identities in order to find what we have lost. How else can we explain the 1994 cover of *Time Magazine* darkening the face of O.J. Simpson in order to portray him as a brutal bogeyman? At that time, Mr. Simpson had been found innocent of the crime of murder; what is the message about the identity of a famous hero who is now reduced to a brute? If you blacken him, do you immediately throw away the heroic quality? And what does one do with a coal-black man? That is, how do you blacken him more? In so doing, are you suggesting that something of the real human is destroyed by blackening?

In 1865, when Africans were finally freed — physically that is -- there was no fitting therapy for the four and a half million people who were now out on the streets and roads of the American South. I mean, no one came to the African people saying that after 250 years of enslavement there needed to be a period of reshaping identities, questioning of spaces (internal and external), accentuating the core, and of keeping pace with the social and political developments that were going on in the rest of the country. After all, whites had already reached California and the Forty-Niners were deep into the pits of the gold mines or panning it along the Russian, American, and other canals and rivers in the Sutter Mill region. Africans were not to see the economic benefit of obtaining mines, ranches, and grazing lands for years to come. In fact, the 250 years of grievous deprivation had come to represent a deficit in the bank account of justice; Martin Luther King, Jr., would take up this metaphor during the March on Washington.

This book, by a brilliant author, is a work of precision and insight. What

Ronald Jackson has intelligently accomplished in this book is advancing the notion that one can negotiate cultural identity based upon the cultural spaces one occupies. His research base is college students, and he has culled such insight from what the respondents have communicated to him that he is perhaps at the forefront of identity research based on empirical evidence.

What is challenged by the way that Ronald Jackson articulates his ideas is the old belief that cultural identities do not change. He is clearly on the side of the negotiated self-definition and sees everyday communicative experiences as fundamental to the way we intensify and extensify our individual sense of personhood within the spaces we share with others. If I am unaware of my own identity or its changing nature I am prevented from knowing whether or not your identity is static or dynamic. I must be engaged with myself in order to be truly engaged with someone else. This is the principal path to enlightenment and to the most conceivable relationship which consists of harmony, justice, balance, and well-being. I am all that I need to be when I am involved in the process of becoming and the process to become; this is the most ancient of ambitions. I have read Ronald Jackson's work with fascination at the varied manifestations of our sense of human achievement, and I know that those who read this work, and are committed to understanding the crucible of race in America, will benefit from its intellectual direction, great sense, and fine scholarship.

Molefi Kete Asante

Preface: Know Thyself

In the forthcoming century, the only thing that is certain to me is that our greatest challenge as a nation will be that of identity. By identity, I mean the process and manner in which individuals, groups, communities, cultures, and institutions define themselves. Whether one chooses to reflect on or dismiss the conversation on identity is unimportant. The fact is that our identities are as constant as the ritualistic rising of the sun and the advent of a new day. What is fascinating to me is to examine why people choose to join or disjoin the discussion of identity. Also, once the topic has arisen, why do many of those who claim to be so well-versed on the issue find themselves "tripped up" on the question of race as it pertains to identity? Equally as intriguing are the instances in which individuals have never reflected on their composite cultural identities and, hence find themselves "lost" in the discussion and in life. Furthermore, these persons often seem well-equipped with repartee which functions to justify their wandering existences. Comments like "I don't think it's necessary to identify yourself as part of a certain culture," or "I have never really had the need to consider it" become part of the echoed battery of responses.

My interest in writing this manuscript emanated from two basic questions that I've been asking myself for years -- who am I, and what does it mean to be American? I've concluded that the former question, is so broad that to answer it completely and without reservation is to have figured the riddle of life. I have never been able to get a suitable response regarding the latter question from myself nor anyone else. One focus group interviewee, from the over-arching research study presented in this book, responded by referring to apple pie and *Brady Bunch* reruns. Others have suggested that being American is being free to be whoever you want to be. But after the media blitz directed at Tiger Woods and the resulting public endorsement of and concomitant relief about his feeling that he is more than just Black, but Cablasian; I immediately wonder where we are headed. A few years ago Mariah Carey, a popular, light-complected rhythm and blues singer, openly claimed that she was not Black. Her refusal to claim a

Black heritage left a stain in the minds of many in the Black community because of her public status and her visible racial features. The obvious questions are, "Just because someone says they are or are not part of a given culture, does that make it so? Who really decides?"

These inquiries are the catalysts for the dialogue on the "negotiation of cultural identity." Perhaps these queries are more specifically concerned with the negotiation of *intra*-cultural identity. This book, however, is about intercultural identity negotiation. In particular, I examine the cultural identity "spaces" of African American (Black) and European American (White) persons. I am very much aware that there are several kinds of identities with which humans can be associated, and several of these are explained in Chapter 2.

I have heard all of my life that White people don't have to change who they are, how they talk, or how they behave. Therefore, I was left with the impression that it was everyone else's responsibility to attempt to adopt the cultural and social personalities of White people. Before this book was written, I had not discovered any published empirical evidence that testified to the intuitive claim that Whites, members of the so-called dominant culture, need not alter their self-definitions. Now that one monograph (this one) has appeared which provides evidence of this commonly held belief, perhaps we can find ways that this conundrum can be further explored and ultimately resolved. In a society that claims to be progressive, diverse and just, we are constantly at the brink of social incohesion, racial antipathy, and political mayhem. In Chapter 3, you will read about several well-respected theorists who advanced philosophies of hatred and superiority. Even recent conversations surrounding Ebonics have attempted to relegate this language of Black people to an inferior status, while the standard form of English is heralded as being "normal," "appropriate," "proper," and "necessary." Each chapter in this book seeks to examine the literature, methods, and limitations of identity research and to determine how committed cultural researchers may adequately prepare for the next millennium, and how -- as the Egyptian step pyramid of Giza encourages -- you, as an individual, may come to "know thyself."

Essentially, this book is a challenge to all of those who know, do not know, or are still trying to know who they are. It is a thinkpiece dedicated to the courageous ones, who frequently confront themselves not only in the mirror of the mind, but also in the mirror of the soul. Also, it is one of the first efforts toward producing a communication theory about the fluctuating nature of human interaction, cultural self-definition and identity development.

In the writing of this book, I have received tremendous encouragement and valued critical feedback from my wife, Ricci, and my other intellectual sparring partners, Bradford Hogue and Tyrome Smith. Certainly, my parents, Sharon Prather, Ronald Jackson, Sr., and Georgia Jackson, as well as my siblings, Bruce, Tishaun, and Tita have all been watchful and supportive. Additionally, I am indebted to the human communication studies faculty of Howard University, as well as the institutional review boards and offices of multicultural affairs of the universities, from whom the respondents were pulled for the study; they are located in the D.C. and New Orleans areas. I have omitted their names here for the sake of the respondents' anonymity. I thank the focus group interview and survey participants from each of the respective schools. I am deeply grateful for the patience and editorial counsel of the book's publisher (Greenwood Press) and each of the editors, including Catherine Lyons. Finally, I am also grateful for the copying services of Shippensburg and Xavier Universities as well as Carroll Community College, each of whom made their resources available to me during the book's completion.

This book is specially dedicated to my daughter, Niyah Simone Jackson whose name means purpose and whose spirit is that of peace.

Chapter 1

Exploring the Need To Be:
An Introduction

> It is a peculiar sensation, this double-consciousness this sense of always
> looking at one's self through the eyes of others, of measuring one's soul
> by the tape of the world that looks on in amused contempt and pity. One
> ever feels his twoness -- an American, a Negro; two souls, two thoughts,
> two unreconciled strivings; two warring ideals in one dark body, whose
> dogged strength alone keeps it from being torn asunder. (W.E.B. Du Bois,
> 1903)

In the early 1900s, W.E.B. Du Bois (1903) predicted the "problem of the
twentieth century as the problem of the color line" and spoke of ideas related to
race, identity, and dual consciousness -- a divided sense of self among African
Americans. One with a dual consciousness traverses borders of Black and
White, never fixed in either identity locale, constantly en route to the other
position. Cornel West (1993) provides a clear description of dual consciousness
as the consequence of being caught between "a quest for white approval and
acceptance, and an endeavor to overcome the internalized association of
blackness with inferiority" (p.18). In brief, Du Bois concerned himself with
terms which would later be identified as accommodation, acculturation,
assimilation, code switching, nigrescence, worldview, and extended identity
(Allport, 1954; Bernstein, 1966; Cross, 1971; Ibrahim and Kahn, 1987;
Nichols, 1976).

The notion of self-division and its consequences has persisted since Du
Bois' statement in 1903, well into the 1960's, and beyond (Allport, 1954; Ani,
1994; Clark and Clark, 1947; Fanon, 1967; Stoddard, 1920; Ting-Toomey,
1989; Wilson, 1978; Woodson, 1933). "The question," Charles Silberman
(1964) writes, "is not whether race differences exist, it is what they mean."
Grier and Cobbs (1968) maintain that there is a constant sense of anxiety
endured by African Americans having constantly to constrict their behaviors,
lifestyles, and language usage in order to function "successfully" within specific

cultural contexts. The same year, the National Advisory Commission on Civil Disorders reported, "Our nation is moving toward two societies, one Black, one White, separate and unequal." This statement mirrored Swedish scholar Gunnar Myrdal's (1944) assessment of racial and socioeconomic imparity offered twenty-four years earlier and that prognosis still remains true even in the 1990's (Hacker, 1992). In 1967, Frantz Fanon, a renowned Psychiatrist, devoted an entire manuscript to the issue of Black identity and labeled it *Black Skin, White Masks*. Fanon (1967) interpreted the condition of the African as one in which the "Black soul is the White man's artifact" (p.14). He posits that to speak is to exist for the other (p.17), which has become a trained choice for the African descendant, since she has "epidermalized" her inferiority. Fanon explains the problem as follows:

The Negro enslaved by his [her] inferiority, the White man enslaved by his superiority alike behave in accordance with a neurotic orientation . . . the Negro having been made inferior, proceeds from humiliating insecurity through strongly voiced self-accusation to despair. (p.60)

After having explained the effects of this dual consciousness, Fanon continues by suggesting that post colonial ontology is designed to explain the human condition from the vantage of the White man; therefore "others" existences are only validated via whiteness (p.110). This, he says, "creates a mass psychoexistential complex." Finally, Fanon indicates Hegel's (1899/1956) philosophical contentions regarding self-consciousness. Hegel posits that consciousness of self is a dependent and interactive phenomenon. Fanon presents a description:

As long as he [she] has not been effectively recognized by the other, that other will remain the theme of his actions. . . in order to win the certainty of oneself, the incorporation of the concept of recognition is essential . . . When it encounters resistance of the other, self-consciousness undergoes the experience of desire.   As soon as I desire, I am asking to be considered. He who is reluctant to recognize me opposes me. In a savage struggle I am willing to accept convulsions of death, in-vincible dissolution, but also the possibility of the impossible. (pp. 216-218)

This passage gives reason for the necessity for African Americans to negotiate their identities on a daily basis, and speaks to the question as to whether European Americans need to do the same. This question is answered two-and-a-half decades later by Pajaczkowska and Young (1992), who deny an identity negotiation imperative for European Americans. They reveal that an identity based on superiority and socioeconomic power never has to develop self-consciousness or succumb to limitations except as these are perceived by the other. Vernon Dixon (1976) supports this hypothesis. Dixon introduces the White cultural assimilation thesis, in which "White America" attempts to equate White culture with American culture, denying all others the same opportunity to equate their cultures with being American. Dixon writes:

In contrast, the ethnic and American identities of Afro-Americans are not the same. Black culture is radically different from White American culture. . . Black Americans

have a sense of 'twoness,' a sense of dual membership, a double consciousness. . .
How do Black people resolve this conflict? Do they deny both these identities,
assert affinity with both, or assert affinity with one and deny the other? No wonder
why Black people, quite rationally, at times feel crazy or unreal in their White
environment of single consciousness, single identity, and single membership. (pp.
32-34)

The questions that Dixon poses reflect an identity challenge that African
Americans answer on a frequent basis in an almost spontaneous and reflexive
manner (Wilson, 1978). Several scholars believe that the level of identity
maturity is the principal characteristic which determines the extent of identity
maintenance (Cross, 1971; White and Parham, 1990; Wilson, 1978; 1990;
1993) . A noteworthy addition to the literature regarding the dialectical nature
of Black existence, identity development and maintenance is that of Cross's
nigrescence model for Black identity development, better known as the "negro-
to-Black conversion" model. This approach, while it does not demonstrate the
process of identity negotiation or development interculturally, establishes a way
of understanding how a "deculturalized" individual becomes revitalized and
increasingly identifies with self and culture. "Nigrescence" is a French word
meaning "to become Black." Consequently, Cross is describing an identity
process experienced by Black people, who undergo a metamorphosis from
whiteness to blackness, or from Negro to Black.

A few years following the advent of Cross' celebrated nigrescence paradigm
in 1971, Edwin Nichols (1976) decided to place cultures and their consistencies
in a theoretical framework which examined cross-cultural differences; as a result,
he created one of the first comprehensive worldview publications. He originally
called his model "The psychological aspects of cultural differences" model.
Presently, it is referred to as "The philosophical aspects of cultural differences"
model, and is used quite frequently for consultation with both public and private
industry organizations throughout the world. The amount of worldview
publications increased during this decade and the next (Asante, 1978;1980;1987;
Carter and Helms, 1987; Dixon, 1976; Fine et al., 1985; Ibrahim and Kahn,
1987; Myers, 1988; X, McGee, Nobles, and Weems, 1975). In the 1990's,
most of the literature on African American identity is dispersed throughout
disciplines such as Psychology, Sociology, and increasingly within
Communication. White and Parham (1990) issued a second edition of Cross's
first work entitled *The Psychology of Blacks: An Afro-American Perspective.*
This comprehensive guide to the Black personality examines "ethnic" identity,
its development and maintenance, and worldview, among other issues. In the
Communication discipline, Hecht, Collier and Ribeau (1993) provide one of the
first volumes ever written in the discipline on African American communication
as it relates to interpretations of African American identity. Their work
thoroughly purviews the psychological, anthropological and social scientific
perspectives taken on this topic, and ends with a communication theory of
ethnic identity. This paradigm shift provides a unique way of examining ethnic
identity by stating that "identity is relational [and a communication
phenomenon]." The basic theoretical stance of the theory is that "identity is
inherently a communication process, and must be understood as a transaction in
which messages are exchanged." The authors offer a challenge I accept here.

The challenge was stated as such: "If identities are negotiated in everyday conversation and if identity negotiation is a process, then we need much more information about the negotiation process itself" (p.173).

It is one of the primary aims of this research study to provide some insight into the process of identity negotiation. Specifically, this research will involve the examination of cultural identity as a relationally-driven negotiation process. This study empirically tests the words of Hecht, Collier and Ribeau, who indicate that "identity is defined by the individual and is co-created as people come into contact with one another and the environment. As people align themselves with various groups this co-creation process is negotiated" (p. 30).

Prior research has not specifically labeled, nor critically examined this process of altering and exchanging interpretations of cultural reality - negotiation of identity. Furthermore, current understanding of this phenomenon assumes either an anthropological or a social psychological posture, rather than a communication perspective of identity transference. Finally, it is critical that European Americans be subjected to the same scientific examination as "other" cultural groups when considering issues of racial, ethnic, and cultural identity.

PURPOSE OF THE RESEARCH

The fundamental purpose of this investigation is to gain further insight into the process of cultural identity negotiation. To negotiate identity implies that identity formation be considered a communication phenomenon among two or more individuals that is driven by message exchange over a period of time. Intuitively, it would seem that European Americans do not find it necessary to define who they are culturally. Additionally, it seems that reasons for entering a negotiation of cultural identity might differ between European American (EA) and African American (AA) students. Context is often identified as a major determining factor in identity shifting. Therefore this study proposes a cross-cultural and cross-situational analysis. European Americans at two predominant-ly African American colleges (Pacifica and Arctica universities), and African Americans at two predominantly European American colleges (Atlantica and Antarctica universities) constitute the sample population.

Specifically the research intends: to gather, analyze, and describe data regarding the relational aspects of cultural identity negotiation; to explore the extent to which African Americans and European Americans feel the need to define themselves culturally; to identify factors which influence cultural identity negotiation; to indicate any differences in cultural identity negotiation among both cultures; and finally, to analyze data received discussing consequences, motivations, and duration of cultural identity negotiation.

STATEMENT OF THE PROBLEM

Slugoski and Ginsburg (1989) assert in their explanation of ego identity that the paradox of personal identity is that at any moment we are the same as, and yet different from the persons we once were or ever will be. This is very similar to the African proverb: "You never step in the same river twice." These statements best characterize the nature and significance of this study. Hecht et al. (1993) speak of changing and shifting ethnic identities. Both culture and the negotiation of cultural identity were described as [on-going] processes. As one moves back and forth among cultural identities or worldviews, adjusting values and behaviors, either voluntarily or involuntarily across space and time, the individual is the same as before, yet affected permanently by this process of cultural identity-alteration, becoming also quite different from before.

Some researchers recommend a balance between both the African and European cultural identities, and further assert that complete denial of either frame of reference will restrict alternatives, choices, interaction, personal growth, and financial security (Ogbonnaya, 1994; Samaj, 1981; West, 1993; White and Parham, 1990).   As aforementioned, Fanon (1967) argues for an essential dialectic among Blacks and Whites which is created in order to locate one's identity. As a result, the "I" (i.e. Blacks) can only determine who the "I" is by identifying who the "other" (i.e. Whites) is and being confirmed by that "other." The problematic is best presented by Pajaczkowska and Young (1992) who assert that whiteness is an absent center, meaning that whites do not find it necessary to define themselves, culturally. These scholars proclaim, "An identity based on power never has to develop consciousness of itself as responsible, it has no sense of its limits except as these are perceived in opposition to others." The profundity of this statement lies in the recognition that the other's identity (self-definition) is an unknown. Yet, the "I" is basing its identity on being recognized by the "other." Consequently, an identity shift from "I" to the "other" is unproductive. In coping with this exhaustive identity shifting, Okechukwu Ogbonnaya (1994) recommends an africentric remedy to the seeming lack of perspective rendered by an identity in motion. He recommends understanding the person as an *intrapsychic community*. In this community, several selves reside, and must do so harmoniously in order to avoid chaos and psychological disorder. Each self exists, not in competition with other selves, but as a collective which appreciates the differences each offers. This interplay mirrors the movement and rhythm of life that must be present in any community, and is necessary for psychological, spiritual, and physical health.

The question is, however, do European Americans, when placed outside of their cultural context feel compelled to alter their behaviors (i.e. codeswitch) and negotiate their cultural identities, or is this just a marginalized group phenomenon?

Starosta and Olorunnisola's (Chen and Starosta, 1998) meta-model for "negotiation of a third culture" provides the most provocative illustration of the choices and consequences of cultural identity shifting, with a potential "separation from primary culture" as the end result. In an attempt to anticipate and resolve objections regarding socioeconomic inequity, the two metatheorists list the third party roles and potential effects of the third culture arrangement. Yet, Starosta and Olorunnisola (Chen and Starosta, 1998) merely suggest issues of sociocultural or economic imparity among the interlocutors; and the authors further contend that a process by which two interactants become creators of a hybrid "third culture," and abandon their primary cultures is ideal.

The research here offers a test of just that. The following tenets undergird the motivation for this investigation:

1.   Negotiating and shifting cultural identities is a communication phenomenon

(Hecht et al., 1993). It seemed that the authors were really talking about shifting multiple identities within daily interactions. Yet, it can still occur laterally, from one culture to another. Negotiation occurs during interaction, and may be the result of one's feelings of submissiveness to another who possesses more power; or it could be simply a reaction to societal norms and expectations.

2.   The shift arises out of the need to communicate with others, and then have those others validate who one is (Fanon, 1967; Madhubuti, 1992). Hecht, Collier, and Ribeau call this co-creation of identity (p. 30).

3.   Identity negotiation precedes identity shifts, and both decisions strongly impact one's decision to consider sacrifice of one worldview (or reality interpretation) in exchange for another.

4.   Even when one *becomes* the other or another (i.e. separates from primary culture), there are still remnants of one's prior self, so although one has changed, one still remains the same. This is one way that the cultural representatives rationalize their decisions to negotiate and shift their cultural identities.

Outline of Problematics

Eight problematics have been identified with identity studies, and help to support the necessity for research such as this. The weight of this investigation lies in responding to the noted voids and inconsistencies, and replacing them with a paradigm shift for examining issues of cultural identity. The problematics are as follows:

1.   Very little research suggests that identity is a negotiation process, except acculturation studies, which fail to recognize that once an individual becomes acculturated, the process continues.

2.   Cultural identity is rarely seen as a transactional communication phenomenon.

3.   The Third Culture Model shows little regard for relational asymmetry among different cultural representatives.

4.   The Third Culture Model considers the creation of a third culture to be ideal.

5.   The communication theory of ethnic identity broadly describes issues of cultural identity, so that it can also account for ethnic groups.

6.   Too many identity studies focus on outcome or process, as opposed to examining both, outcome and process.

7.   There is not a clear distinction in the identity literature between racial, ethnic and cultural identity.

8.   Acculturation, accommodation, and adaptation may appear to be congruent terms to describe the negotiation of cultural identity, but they are not.

THEORETICAL FRAMEWORK

Having duly noted that negotiation of cultural identity is a process involving the modification of one's interpretation of reality (i.e. worldview), the present study adopts one metatheory and a recent communication theory of cultural identity as its theoretical framework. These paradigms are Starosta and Olorunnisola's (Chen and Starosta, 1998) "Third Culture Building" metatheory and Hecht et al.'s (1993) "Communication Theory of Ethnic Identity," respectively. Hecht et al.'s communication theory of ethnic identity is interpreted as a communication theory of cultural identity because the authors' definition of ethnicity is parallel to this investigation's definition of culture. These two paradigms were selected to support this research, since the former is a model which epitomizes negotiation as a communication phenomenon, and the latter is a theory which recognizes the connection between communication and cultural identity. Only certain applicable components of each paradigm are explained within this chapter. For a more thorough explanation of each, see Chapter 5.

Third Culture Building

Third Culture Building (TCB) was initiated by William Starosta and Anthony Olorunnisola (Chen and Starosta, 1998), and thus far has not been empirically tested or verified. This nascent metatheory is most applicable within this study since it encompasses several gradations ranging from micro (individual) to macro (societal) levels of communication analysis. The TCB model identifies these levels of communication analysis as intracultural, interpersonal, rhetorical, and mass media. The present study's conception of negotiation of cultural identity is directed by a process-oriented approach to identity exploration. Starosta and Olorunnisola (Chen and Starosta, 1998) add depth to the process, and explain the interactive nature of meaning construction. The authors suggest that this interaction process can be either voluntary or coerced, with ephemeral or enduring effects, across or within national boundaries. The model's design includes ten temporally arranged stages, and is presented in detail in chapter five.

Communication Theory of Ethnic Identity

This paradigm was established with the premise that African Americans are an ethnic group however it is not limited to the study of African Americans. The theory is derived from the accumulated research of its authors. For example, Collier and Thomas's (1988) *cultural identity theory* proposed the relationship between intercultural competence and cultural identity -- a central feature of the communication theory of ethnic identity. Hecht, Collier and Ribeau (1993) provide an heuristic contribution to the discipline of intercultural communication by applying this linkage to African Americans. Moreover, the expansion of Collier and Thomas's theory included an interpretation of African American identity based on core symbols, prescriptions, code, conversation, and community.   This theory, like Starosta and Olorunnisola's third culture building, is fully explained in chapter five.

RESEARCH QUESTIONS

Four research questions have been created to illustrate the problem of the study. By utilizing the Third Culture Model and the Communication theory of Ethnic Identity which structure the framework for the study, the following questions are investigated:

1.   What similarities and differences were reported in the way that European American and African American students define themselves culturally?

2.   What are the similarities and differences in the process of cultural identity negotiation among European American and African American students?

3.   How   does   negotiation   of   cultural   identity   pose   long-term identity consequences for European American and African American respondents?

4.   Under   what   conditions   do   European   American   and African   American respondents feel the need to reconsider their cultural identities?

DEFINITION OF TERMS

Before continuing, it is imperative to define conceptually a few of the key terms that have been used so frequently thus far -- race, ethnicity, culture, identity, negotiation, cultural identity, and negotiation of cultural identity.

First, it is important to note that ethnic identity is not the preferred term here, since it might be confused with its etymological root in Medieval English, *ethnik* or the Latin *ethica* meaning "heathen" (Asante, 1990; Stebbins, 1992). Moreover, ethnicity is regarded as a sub-cultural group membership often relating to racial, linguistic or religious affiliation only. The terms ethnicity and culture too often appear in the literature as synonymous terms; therefore this research supports the position of Molefi Asante (1980; 1987; 1990), who cautions investigators against using these terms uncritically. Asante (1990, p. 28) suggests that the primary concern with using the word "ethnic" within cultural studies is its eurocentric bias, as it relates to such scholarly endeavors as ethnomusicology or ethnomethodology. These become studies of "the other" or the "heathen" (Non-European). This tends to preclude any European from claiming membership in an ethnic group or possessing ethnicity as a personality descriptor, since they are not "the other." It is a tendency of these European researchers to provide an emic (subjective, in-group) analysis from an etic (objective, out-group) perspective and to disqualify themselves from any ethnic group memberships. This investigation is an emic examination of African American identity from an emic perspective. The logic of making this point is not to say that cultural studies of one culture cannot be done by individuals of other cultures, but rather that they should be approached with a sensitivity to cultural relevancy and accuracy. By imposing an out-group perspective on an in-group, hegemony arises, and the study loses much of its significance (Asante, 1990). To avoid this, emic analyses must be conducted from an emic perspective. One such emic analysis is that of identity. Before conducting a cultural analysis of identity, however, I must critically distinguish the terms, race, ethnicity, and culture. (For further discussion of terms, see Chapter 3.)

Race is historically understood as a categorization of people based on biological characteristics. Anthropologists have devised hundreds of divisions known as racial groups. Three of the most popular racial descriptions are Negroid, Caucasoid, and Mongoloid (Montagu, 1962). *Ethnicity* is a social construct created to define group memberships within cultures; group memberships associated with race, language, and religion are often characterized as ethnic groups. Social differences and the disconnectedness from a geographical location are the primary conditions that distinguish ethnicity from culture (Stebbins, 1992). *Culture* is a term used to describe a set of patterns, beliefs, behaviors, institutions, symbols, and practices shared and perpetuated by a consolidated group of individuals connected by an ancestral heritage and a concomitant geographical reference location (Ani, 1994; Diop, 1991; Holloway, 1990; Levine, 1977; Nobles, 1986). Sub-cultural groups, such as those related to age, gender, sexual preference, and the physically challenged are not to be identified as cultures. As previously mentioned, critical use and examination of these terms is mandatory for any scholarly analysis of cultural identity.

Within this study, *identity* is that which confers a sense of self or personhood. It also refers to self-definition. The author contends that there is a direct relationship between identity and one's ability to define self. Identity is found within messages communicated in daily interaction. Every definition of self includes culture. Wade Nobles's (1986) definition of *culture* is "a process which gives people a general design for living and patterns for interpreting their reality." Nobles (1986) offers a worldview explanation of culture that he grounds in behavior, value, and attitudes. Specific to this investigation, culture is also defined as a set of patterned behaviors, norms, roles, meanings, rituals, rules, and ways of communicating, which are reflective of worldview. Linda James Myers (1991) argues that worldview should not be ruled out as a viable instrument for assessing identity. She claims that members of the dominant culture may be unaware of their non-acceptance of true cultural differences. This may be the result of mistaking the ease and competency with which non-dominant cultural members codeswitch, with a genuine coalescence or sense of compatibility. She further explains that dominant cultural members may never become fully acquainted with "other" cultures due to a lack of understanding of how those others relate to the world. *Worldview* is defined as a set of philosophical assumptions, values, beliefs, and orientations toward the world that ultimately determine how one defines self; and where one places his or her locus of control. Worldview studies have been instrumental in facilitating intercultural relations, and have a potentially tremendous contribution among interpretive communication studies of cultural identity. Cultural identity is still defined from a communication perspective, but is more closely linked to a discussion of cultural worldview. *Cultural identity* can only be explained by considering the link between self-definition and worldview. It relates to the extent to which one is a representative of a given culture behaviorally, communicatively, psychologically, and sociologically. By controlling one's own self-definition, one maintains the ability to determine one's agenda (i.e. goals), and ultimately their destiny. *Negotiation* is a bargaining process in which two or more individuals consider the exchange of ideas, values, and beliefs. The consequence can be either distributive (win-lose) or integrative (win-win). *Negotiation of cultural identity* is a process in which one considers the gain, loss, or exchange of their ability to interpret their own reality or worldview. If it is discovered that one has negotiated part or all of her cultural identity, then that can be translated to mean that she has conceded a dimension of her cultural locus of control. As a natural consequence of this negotiation, it can be argued that she has also, in the process, forfeited certain cultural values, traditions and/or norms (which serve to define who she is) within that communication episode.

Ani (1994) considers several characteristics of the "phenomenon of culture," three of which are pertinent to this research: the phenomenon of culture provides a worldview which defines culture for its members; it creates a sense of collective cultural identity; and it provides for the creation of shared symbols and meanings which form a collective conscious. Ani further explains that ideology and culture are inseparable.   Hecht, Collier, and Ribeau (1993) speak of this same concept of culture but label it differently, the name given to this is ethnic culture. It is described as the unique and shared characteristic of a community with a common sense of ancestry, tradition, aesthetics, perceptions and values that coalesce around racial attributes. From the explanations given, this study proposes the definition of *cultural identity* as the sense of belonging to a cultural community that reaffirms self or personhood for the individual and is created by: the people, their interactions, and the context in which they relate. Cultural identity is comprised of values, mores, meanings, customs, and beliefs used to relate to the world; it continually defines what it was, what it is, and what it is becoming. This statement supports Hecht et al.'s idea of the movement and fluctuation of identity. Thus, when speaking of the *negotiation of cultural identity,* this investigation is additionally referring to the process in which two or more individuals place aspects of their cultural identities in a bargaining context, voluntarily or involuntarily, as goods to be negotiated. The assumption is that one does not negotiate unless he or she is willing to make an exchange (whether equal or unequal) of some kind and that, at certain times and with certain persons, the process occurs out of necessity, and at other times with others it is voluntary. Overall, however, the *negotiation of cultural identity* involves the exchange or relinquishment of an interpretation of reality that serves to define self. This occurs above and below levels of consciousness; however the present study will only analyze the conscious exchange process. It is precisely the ingredients of culture that determine that with which cultural members identify and can potentially negotiate.

Finally, Horton and Hunt (1964) propose four functions of culture: to define situations; to define attitudes, values, and goals; to identify myths, legends, and heroes; and to identify appropriate patterns of behavior. When discussing cultural identity negotiation, its functions are an integral part.   One is negotiating the ability to maintain a cultural sense of self in any given situation. This involves the decision as to whether to rearrange attitudes, values, and goals; to redefine myths, legends, and heroes; and/or to alter one's behavior. Perhaps the latter function is of greatest consequence in the overall negotiation process, since the selection of appropriate patterns is based primarily upon the interactant's understanding of what it means to be normal.

SIGNIFICANCE OF THE RESEARCH

The significance of the research presented is in what it offers in advancing identity studies. Very few studies have systematically examined both African American students in a European American educational context and European American students in an African American educational context. The variation in context may reveal similarities and differences previously undiscovered. Also, the conceptual development of identity studies as they relate to culture, negotiation and communication confirms the need for this study. First, in the few studies that do regard the linkage between culture and identity as a process, the metamorphosis is described as a gradual development from either Blackness to Whiteness, or Whiteness to Blackness. This ignores the actual back-and-forth movement between the two polar positions, while emphasizing outcome as opposed to process. Other studies have done just the opposite, accentuated process, and not the outcome. This study endorses examining both, process and outcome. Second, the research uncovers European Americans' perceptions of their own identity. Third, Starosta and Olorunnisola's (Chen and Starosta, 1998) Third Culture Building metatheory is being empirically tested for the first time. Fourth, this is one of the first studies to empirically consider Hecht, Collier and Ribeau's Communication Theory of Ethnic Identity. Finally, the research reveals an interpretive and functionalist analysis of the negotiation of cultural identity.

By offering a triangulated perspective for the consideration of cultural identity as a negotiation process, previously unavailable data is provided. This data will facilitate an improved understanding of European American and African American identity, as well as behavioral and cultural code switching. Furthermore, the influence of context as a determining factor of an identity shift imperative will be recognized. The sample population is unique in that it is comprised of European American and African American students in the "other-race" context. The research also makes general suggestions for individuals, groups, organizations, and institutions interested in issues of code switching, racism, self-definition, cultural identity, and worldview.

METHODOLOGY

Clifford Geertz (1973) advises that a "thick description" be used for gathering and interpreting cultural data for social scientific research. This implies that an interpretive analysis be implemented, in which in-group participants provide a set of explanations concerning in-group phenomena. Fred Kerlinger (1986), however argues effectively for a triangulated approach, which considers both, the interpretive and functionalist paradigms. Focus group interviewing is an excellent interpretive method for discovering beliefs and attitudes that undergird human behavior. The data is richer since each participant introduces a different perspective that, when communicated, may encourage another participant to share additional experiences. The group format elicits an interactivity and compels the participants to expound in instances where they might not have done so. Moreover, this technique is especially valuable when seeking information regarding complex experiences and/or intricate consequences of human interaction. The focus group technique is instrumental in this study due to its unrestrictive nature. There are no a priori categories, yet every researcher reserves certain bias. This method does not eliminate that bias, but it does allow the participants to elaborate on various issues, as opposed to a quantitative technique which generalizes across situations, space, and time. The secondary study utilizing the survey instrument is quantitative in its approach, but is only used to verify the results of the primary study employing focus group interviews.

African American students at predominantly European American colleges (Atlantica and Antarctica universities) and European American students at predominantly African American colleges (Pacifica and Arctica universities) will comprise the sample population. Focus groups typically include eight to twelve members. The two colleges from which the sample population for the interviews were drawn were Pacifica and Atlantica universities. The 14-item survey was distributed to students at Arctica and Antarctica universities.

There were six students participating in each focus group, and fifteen students completing surveys from each of the aforementioned colleges (an adequate sample size considering the parent population).

ORGANIZATION OF THE BOOK

Chapter 1, *Exploring the Need To Be: An Introduction*, encompasses the background, statement of the problem, identity perspectives, theoretical framework, research questions, definition of terms, purpose and significance of the research, and finally, the methodology.

Chapter 2, *Overview of Identities Negotiated Within Interaction*, is a comprehensive review of the literature addressing distinctions and conceptual beginnings of race, ethnicity, and culture. Also included in this chapter is a purview of the perspectives concerning identity, worldview and culture held by sociologists, psychologists, and communication scholars.

Chapter 3, *Origins: A Foundation for the Discussion of Race in America*, is a comprehensive review of the literature addressing distinctions and conceptual beginnings of race, ethnicity, and culture.

Chapter 4, *Racial, Ethnic and Cultural Identities: An Interdisciplinary Perspective*, provides evidence of a comprehensive understanding of identity studies; illustrates the foundational studies setting the groundwork for this one; and demonstrates the heuristic value of this investigation and its place among prior identity research.

Chapter 5, *Two Theories of Communicated Identity*, is unique because it showcases two indigenous [to the discipline] communication paradigms which theorize about the operation of identity within human interaction.

Chapter 6, *Research Design and Methodology*, presents the research questions, explains and defends the methodological framework, and delineates the research design and procedures employed. The composition and selection criteria for both, the surveyed sample and the focus group respondents, is explained, followed by a justification for the focus group technique employed.

Chapter 7, *When "The Other" Is White: Cultural Identity and Sensemaking*, presents the findings of the study. Several themes from the survey and comments from the focus group interviews are revealed in order to mark the consistency of responses from using both methods. The findings related to the feedback from the interviews is considered the primary study, while the analysis associated with the survey responses is identified as the secondary study.

Chapter 8, *The Results and Synthesis*, provides a systematic review of the entire book by summarizing the purpose, objectives, literature, research questions, methods, results, implications, and the heuristic value of studying cultural identity negotiation.

Chapter 2

Overview of Identities Negotiated Within Interaction

> Every black individual, group, or family is haunted by this "double consciousness" to which Du Bois refers. It is an existential fact of black existence and its influence for better or worse, is pervasive in all areas of black behavior... the man [woman] is a "split personality," a schizoid personality which tries to operate with two sets of mutually incompatible needs, drives, impulses, values, cultural traditions, ways of thinking, etc., simultaneously.... The hallmark of schizoid living is ambivalence, an ambivalence which enters virtually every activity of the schizoid's life.... His life is characterized by a constant vacillation between two conflicting worlds of differing ethnic histories, lifestyles, values, etc. (Wilson, 1978, pp. 51-53)

In the 1910's, W.E.B. Du Bois followed his monumental work on "double consciousness," *Souls of Black Folks,* with a comprehensive survey of an ancestral heritage rooted in Africa entitled *The Negro.* His hope was to resolve the problem of race relations, self-division, and identity negotiation by offering evidence to suggest that both Whites and Blacks shared a common African ancestry, and thus there is only one culture - a "world culture" (Du Bois, 1915). As expected, this world hypothesis was rejected by White historians. Its major influence was the realization that the Egyptian culture as well as the Arabian, Jewish, Roman, and Greek cultures shared a Black foundation. The issue of a dual identity remained unresolved. White nationalists such as Lothrop Stoddard (1920) thoroughly contested such hypotheses, and established other paradigms which sought to confirm White superiority and Black inferiority. Stoddard indicated that Africans were the lowest on the scale of humanity:

> ... the brown and yellow peoples have contributed greatly to the civilization of the world and have profoundly influenced human progress. The Negro, on the contrary, has contributed virtually nothing. Left to himself, he remained a savage, and in the past, his only quickening has been where brown men have imposed their ideas

and altered his blood. . . the black race has never shown real constructive power. . . . there seems to be no reason for this except race. (pp. 100-101)

This work is indicative of the race dominance efforts forwarded by White nationalists, whose mission was to develop a sharp contrast between Whites and the "others." Naturally, the "others" in this case were African descendants in America. African American authors persisted with literature critiquing the condition of African descendants (i.e. Negro, Black, Colored, and later Afro- or African American). Carter G. Woodson's (1933) seminal volume entitled *The Mis-education of the Negro,* is often cited by scholars researching the so-called "problem of the Negro" in an attempt to better understand the condition of African Americans historically, culturally, and psychologically. Dr. Woodson, an acclaimed historian and founder of Black History Month, explains the results of an *educated* dual consciousness or what this investigation labels African American negotiation of identity:

When you control a [hu]man's thinking you do not have to worry about his actions. You do not have to tell him not to stand here or go yonder. He will find his 'proper place' and will stay in it. You do not have to send him to the back door, he will go without being told. In fact, if there is no back door, he will cut one for his special benefit. His education makes it necessary. (Woodson, 1933, p. xiii)

The education that Woodson describes is equivalent to training or conditioning. He later proclaims that the White-dominated system encourages Blacks to be White, and simultaneously convinces Blacks that they will never become White, and the best they will ever be is a good Negro (Woodson, p. 23). In accordance with Woodson's theme of racial accommodation, the Carnegie Commission launched an investigation in the early 1940's of race issues present in the United States with the principal author being Gunnar Myrdal (1944). This project provided a sense of racial progress by soliciting the assistance of several African American scholars such as Sterling Brown, W.E.B. Du Bois, E. Franklin Frazier, Alain Locke, and Ralph Bunche. According to Omi and Winant (1986, p.17) Myrdal's *An American Dilemma* in 1944, marked the rise of the ethnicity paradigm (Kuhn, 1970) which explains that race is a social category or group, and is only one determinant of ethnic identity. Ethnicity was seen as "the result of a group formation process based on culture and descent" (Glazer and Moynihan, 1975, p. 4). Myrdal's (1944) primary challenge was directed toward biologistic theories of race, which sought to sustain race prejudice, inequality, and segregation. The chief debate among the assimilationists and cultural pluralists, within this paradigm, was over the possibility of maintaining racial group identities over time considering the pressure of anglo-conformity (Omi and Winant, 1986). From an historical viewpoint, ethnic identity, africanisms and "carryovers" of African descendants in America were systematically examined by Melville Herskovits, three years prior to Myrdal's work, in 1941. Herskovits (1941), in *The Myth of the Negro Past*, offered evidence to suggest that elements of culture found in the New World were traceable to Africa (Holloway, 1990; Mintz and Price, 1976). He illustrated several West African contributions to American society, and provided a segue into the study of African retentions and distinctiveness. The "myth" that he attempted to destroy was that African descendants were without culture, and therefore without identity, since there was nothing with which they could identify, except their Americanness. In 1947, Kenneth and Mamie Clark executed their monumental study of racial identification among school children. The researchers asked children questions regarding their feelings toward white and Black dolls, such as which was more beautiful or which would you like to play with the most? The findings indicated that Black children had a high degree of self-hatred, believed to be the result of a racially intense and discriminatory society. This experiment had a tremendous impact on the state of scholarly endeavors regarding children and race but, most important to this investigation, is the position it holds among the studies on cultural identity (cultural and racial identity, as terms, will be used interchangeably). In the 1950's, the study of cultural identity moved to another level with the advent of Gordon Allport's (1954) *The Nature of Prejudice*. This study is a classic among the literature on race, discrimination, prejudice, and accommodation. Allport investigates the characteristics of prejudgment, categorization, contact, and tolerance by asking prudent questions such as "can there be an in-group without an out-group?" Furthermore, he enumerates eight different types of cultural contact, and analyzes each while maintaining his focus on cultural prejudice. This study came one decade prior to the well-known "contact hypothesis" (Amir, 1969) which posits that the more one comes in contact with other cultural groups, the lower one's cultural prejudice toward that group will become.

Most of the literature up until the end of the 1950's said very little about African American identity, and especially its negotiation. The scholarship on Black identity was marked by self-hatred hypotheses, and descriptions of self-discomfort, and a quest for human treatment. Literature on Black personality and Black identity did not flourish until the 1960's. E. Franklin Frazier (1963) rebutted the retention views of Melville Herskovits (1941) in his work entitled, *The Negro Church in America*. Frazier contended that Herskovits (1941) expressed too much uncertainty about the extent to which certain elements of African culture have survived, in his *Myth of the Negro Past* . Furthermore, Frazier asserts that "Negroes were practically stripped of their social heritage . . . and exhibit a high degree of cultural homogeneity." (Frazier, 1963). That same year, James Baldwin (1963), in *The Fire Next Time*, proclaimed that conscious Black Americans are in rage almost all the time. This emotional state was described as the consequence of the preceding one-hundred years, dating back to the Emancipation Proclamation of 1863. Baldwin (1963, p. 2) asserted that while no longer being physically brutalized, the condition of the Negro had not changed. Thus he appeals to the relatively conscious Whites and Blacks: "God gave Noah the rainbow sign, No more water, the fire next time !" The unchanging state of Black America at the time was more than discouraging. African Americans could find no justification for being treated this way, and often believed that race dominance would subside with desegregation and the end of slavery. Silbermann (1964, p.73) quotes Kenneth Stampp, a noted historian, as having believed, "Negroes, after all, are only White men with Black skins, nothing more, nothing less." Naturally, works like this one facilitated racial inequality. Throughout the 1960s and into the 1970s and

1980s, ontological questions began to arise in scholarly literature regarding the nature of Black existence (Asante, 1978; Collier and Thomas, 1988; Dixon, 1976; Fanon, 1967; Glazer and Moynihan, 1975; Hare, 1991; Nichols, 1976; Samaj, 1981; White, 1984; Wilson, 1978).

Hare (1991), the coordinator of the country's first African American studies program, discussed, in his *Black Anglo-Saxons,* the plethora of identity presentations offered by, categorizing them as either one or a combination of the following types: dignitaries, image-makers, mimics, cultured, sociables, possessors, exiles, insiders, supercitizens, pioneers, and/or cosmopolitans. These labels are personality descriptors that conceal cultural identity.

Fanon, a renowned psychiatrist, spent much of his time in Martinique, a French Caribbean island, advocating a Black liberation psychology, which would be a vital component in releasing African descendants from an oppressed condition of viewing themselves from a European perspective. His major work, *Black Skin White Masks,* announces a psychological dilemma encountered by Blacks. He declared that the racial juxtaposition of Blacks and Whites causes a massive psychoexistential complex, in which both races become involved in a neurotic orientation toward being recognized by the other. The absence of this necessary recognition refuses validation of the other's identity, and significance of the other's presence.

Glazer and Moynihan (1975) discuss the results of an unrecognized identity, from a sociological perspective. The authors explain that ethnic groups are divided by socially-defined boundaries. Ascribed identity is much more constant, stable, and immutable than voluntary affiliation. Boundaries can be changed within ethnic groups due to the extent of ascriptiveness, cohesion, ethnocentrism, or acculturation into another group. As a result of this alteration, group identities may be lost through what the writers identify as assimilation, amalgamation, or incorporation. Assimilation is the "process of erasing the boundary between one group and another." Amalgamation is the combination of two groups to form a larger and different group, which is similar to Starosta and Olorunnisola's (Chen and Starosta, 1998) TCB model. Incorporation is the third type, which is the sacrifice of one's identity, in order to merge with that of another (Glazer and Moynihan, 1975, p.115). These three methods of losing identity are possibilities for a cultural identity that remains unrecognized.

Nichols (1976) and Asante (1978) agree that there are evident cultural differences between African Americans (Blacks) and European Americans (Whites) that may cause psychological disparity between the two groups. Wilson (1978) expounds on these differences and the apparent psychological disparity by commenting on socioeconomic conditions. He explains that the Black middle class experiences *double consciousness* much more acutely than the Black working or lower class due to a persistent struggle for economic equality. This equality, the Black individual feels can only be achieved by being fully accepted by the white middle class, consequently a social-psychological schizoid behavior ensues. Social-psychological ambivalence becomes the hallmark of this behavior.

Samaj (1981) explicates the duality issue by offering a threefold framework for understanding a Black extended identity, characterized as alien, diffused, and collective identities. The alien is the one who is the most isolated from a cultural sense of self. In other words, this individual would deny an African ancestral linkage or minimize its importance. This person views the world from an individualistic and competitive perspective. The alien would endorse Rene' Descarte's statement, "I think, therefore I am" (cogito ergo sum). The diffused, on the other hand, seek to establish a worldview which appreciates and behaves in accordance with multiple cultural ideologies. This predates Ogbonnaya's (1994) conception of a community of selves which are separate identities that live harmoniously together. Finally, in contrast with the alien is the collective identity. This self-conception is grounded in a traditional African worldview. An individualist conception of reality is a non sequitur. Each person is an extension of the collective, hence Kwame Nkrumah's statement to the All-African People's Revolutionary Party, "None of us are free until all of us are free." The collective identity supports the ideas of Mbiti (1970), who claims, "I am because we are, and because we are, I am."

White and Parham (1990) issued a second edition of White's (1984) first work, *The Psychology of Blacks: An Afro-American Perspective.* This second edition extends the first edition by adding a contemporary perspective to the Black personality, ethnic identity, its development and maintenance, and worldview, among other issues. The authors reject self-hatred hypotheses, and advocate a contextual analysis of the Black self-concept which is responsive to changes over space and time.

Marimba Ani (1994) illustrates that the ideological thrust of culture is inescapable, and therefore must be considered in any cultural analysis. Ideology is characterized as that which shapes personality and behavior, and provides a spiritual and intellectual foundation for group cohesiveness. The interconnection between culture, ideology, and identity lies in a self-definition and ability to determine one's cultural well-being. The African concept of *self*-definition is a collective concept; therefore the self can only be understood as an interdependent component of the whole. In other words, the traditional definition of the self as an individualized identity is inapplicable. Consequently, the ability to define self contributes to the liberation and destiny of the collective. Without understanding of culture, concern for ideology, and control over self-definition, Frantz Fanon's (1967) painstaking prediction may hold true for African Americans, or any marginalized group: "for the Black man there is only one destiny, and it is White" (p. 10).

This concern is echoed by Marimba Ani, who says that Europeans teach a "cultural logic" and worldview "to ordinary participants who assimilate it, assume it, and push it beneath the surface from where it influences their collective behavior and responses" (p.7). One set of those ordinary participants are African Americans, whose behaviors and responses are contextually (or situationally) presented as white masks (Fanon, 1967) but, as Nathan Hare (1991) argues, some ordinary participants never take off the masks, and as a result find them permanently affixed. Then, what is needed, at least in America, is what Ani calls de-Europeanization.

The attempt here is not to establish a framework whereby African Americans can be said to occupy a certain cultural space, and are prohibited from entering others. This research concurs with that of White and Parham (1990), who strongly denounce notions of self-hatred and privilege of race/culture categorization as solutions to the problems with which African American identity is confronted. Nor does the study assert that all African Americans think and behave exactly alike; rather African Americans, as other marginalized groups in America, must concern themselves with the confluence of two distinct cultural realities or worldviews, one being African and the other European.

Often, psychological literature regarding the African American personality explains this in terms of developmental psychological approaches, such as Cross'(1971) nigrescence model. Ani arranges the order of this process accordingly -- mythoform (preconsciousness) to mythology (consciousness) to ideology (self-consciousness). This non-heirarchal achievement of self-consciousness occurs as a result of becoming aware of how mythological systems work to hold one's consciousness constant by creating icons to be instilled in the form of a relatively unconscious collective experience. Thereafter, one is able to arrive at self-definition and control over one's own destiny to whatever human extent that might be possible (Ani, pp. 10-11).

In the Communication discipline, Hecht, Collier and Ribeau (1993) provide one of the first volumes ever written in the discipline on African American communication as it relates to interpretations of African American identity. Much of Collier and Thomas' (1988) rules theory on cultural identity is incorporated in the author's communication theory of ethnic identity. While Hecht et al.'s (1993) work thoroughly purviews the psychological, anthropological, and social scientific perspectives taken on this topic, it concludes with the aforementioned theory. This paradigm shift provides a unique way of examining ethnic identity by stating that "identity is relational [and a communication phenomenon]." The major contribution of the theory is that "identity is inherently a communication process, and must be understood as a transaction in which messages are exchanged" (p.161).

OVERVIEW OF IDENTITY PERSPECTIVES

As is illustrated by the cursory glance of race-related issues offered, many scholars and researchers alike have been fascinated with issues of identity for decades, although there have been some discrepancies as to what this term identity means. The sociological, psychological, and communication perspectives on identity are outlined within this section.

Sociologists define it according to the connectedness between the individual self and the social self. These scholars have been said to consider identity to be an extra-sociological issue (Holzner and Robertson, 1979). Nonetheless, this notion of an interconnectedness between self and society is widely recognized in social psychology, and exemplified in the works of George Herbert Mead, Harold Garfinkel, and Erving Goffman, who are often quoted and classified under the rubric of the ethogenic paradigm of identity in social science (Harre, 1979). Ethogenics or "the New Psychology" is used to describe those social scientific perspectives which seek to discover the methods and belief systems individuals use to assign meaning to their actions and to construct and maintain their identities (Burkitt, 1992). This is a relatively new interpretive framework which also concerns itself with the rules individuals develop to perpetuate or constrict their system of discourse, hence managing and negotiating their identities, as well as interactions with others.

Psychologists explain identity by attaching prefixes to the word, such as personal identity and racial identity. Personal identity relates to one's self-concept, and is manifested in everything from the companion one selects to something as ordinary as the clothes one wears. It is often defined in reference to Sigmund Freud's theory of ego identity, which interprets social reality according to three interdependent parts -- id, ego, and superego. The id is considered the raw form of the human personality which is disconnected from reality, primal and instinctual by nature. It is deemed to be parallel to the unconscious, responding unknowingly, and therefore uncontrollably, to urges, desires, and instincts. The ego is the "I," the active agent in any system of discourse within the internal or external world. When speaking of identity, scholars often refer to the ego as a functioning agent of self-definition. Freud believed that there was a superordinate, organizing nucleus in the human personality, responsible for the connection between the individual and society. This nucleus he named the superego, the socialite of the personality triad, directly influenced by cultural and societal memberships and roles; it informed the ego to behave accordingly. The ego, as the active agent, then operates as an interface between the id and the superego in order to interpret environmental stimuli and determine a course of action. Joel Kovel (1984) explained that when the superego is aligned with certain cultural controls, adaptation has occurred and one becomes "normal." If one exhibits behavior other than what is prescribed by the conventions of the dominant culture, one is deemed "abnormal," thus substantiating a presumed ego-deficiency.

Karl Jung (1961) parted from the Freudian school of psychological analysis to propose a different paradigm for the unconscious and how it manifests itself in the occult, symbolisms, dreams, and myths. Among the list of archetypes Jung offered, three directly pertain to this research -- persona, anima, and the self. Persona allows one to create and maintain a social facade, which creates the illusion of an everyday self. The persona is the masked external representation of one's identity. Anima is derived from the Latin *animus*, meaning spirit. Thus, anima refers to the spiritual forces that govern human action and interaction. (Incidentally, anima is the term used for males, and animus for females.) This is the internal representation of one's identity. Finally, there is the self, which serves as the nucleus in the constellation of principles, mores, values, and beliefs one holds.

Members of the school of African Psychology have a unique perspective, which more readily embraces definitions of identity that accentuate a cultural self-concept. White and Parham (1990, p. 42) support the depiction of identity as including "personal attitudes, feelings, characteristics, and behaviors (personal identity) and the identification with a larger group of people who share those characteristics." This collective heuristic is indicative of the African-centered paradigm. Wade Nobles (1991) in "African Philosophy: Foundations of Black Psychology" asserts that self-definition of African Americans is derived from several cultural and philosophical premises reflected in an africentric worldview. Particularly, the following premises are discussed: religion, philosophy, notions of unity, concept of time, death and immortality, kinship, community, and ethos. Consequently, African Psychology scholars posit that one's ability to define self is directly related to a recognition and understanding of one's cultural worldview.

Still, communication scholars describe identity from a slightly different perspective. Geertz (1973) recommended in *The Interpretation of Cultures* that cultural analyses be conducted from a "thick description," a term borrowed from Gilbert Ryle (1949). In other words, cultural identity is defined in relationship to how one interprets his or her membership in a given culture. The "thickness" refers to the texture and depth given to explanations of in-group activities. A "thin" description is one that can be applied wholecloth, generalizing across space and time, thus referring to the breadth of the explanation. The types of identity discussed in the communication literature include counter-identity and co-identity, as well as social, intergroup, ethnolinguistic, cultural, racial, and ethnic identities. Identities and roles are described by Burke and Tully (1977) metacommunicatively and are classified as counter-identities and co-identities.

Counter-identities are the dialectical relationships enacted by two interlocutors who maintain different roles, such as in a buyer/seller or parent/child relationship. Psychologist Eric Berne, author of *Games People Play*, called these communicative events transactions, and the roles he named scripts or scripted identities. Co-identities are described as having multiple identities that co-exist within a given context. For example, as a politician running for office, you may represent certain groups without even knowing it, such as those related to gender, age, marital status, sexual orientation and race. Burke and Tully were two of the earlier scholars to contend that we not only have multiple identities, but also that these identities present themselves in simultaneous and overlapping ways. Social identity theorists (Berger and Luckmann, 1967; Gergen, 1994; Sarbin and Kitsuse, 1994; Schutz, 1967; Tajfel, 1978; Turner, 1968) would concur that varied roles emerge within social circumstances.

The work of social identity specialists originated under the rubric of social construction of reality. This theory of social reality instructs the research community that meanings, roles, norms, and conventions are the result of active participation in social networks, not the isolated consequence of one individual's conjectures. There is apparent support from sociological research within this paradigm. Harre and Secord's (1972) ethogenic science or ethogeny was borne from the "social constructionist movement; ethogeny concerns itself with describing and defining meaning within a given episode. As mentioned earlier, this assignment of meaning facilitates a certain interpretation of reality. In 1978, Henry Tajfel established social identity theory. Turner (1968) and his notion of social categorization is often credited with the development of this critical model, which explains that a component of one's self-concept matures due to the emotional and political attachments associated with group memberships. Erving Goffman (1959) introduced a similar conception in his notable work *The Presentation of Self in Everyday Life*. In this book Goffman suggested that humans tend to assign themselves to socially recognizable categories and subsequently allow those memberships to define and validate their identities through social interaction. Ethnic groups are just one of these socially recognized categories. The similarities and differences among members of ethnic groups are frequently discussed according to in-groups and out-groups.

It is interesting to note that up until the 1980s (Giles and Johnson, 1981) much of the social scientific research on ethnic group identity was accomplished objectively, without regard for subjective interpretation of human experience (or thick description). The obstacle that arose was that those with either very strong or very weak in-group identities could potentially define communication with the out-group in interpersonal, and not intergroup/intercultural, terms. Intergroup identity has subsequently enjoyed extensive study but has usually been framed as concomitant to social identity, social categorization, and social attribution i.e., stereotyping (Devereux, 1975; De Vos, 1982; Frideres, 1982; Hewstone and Jaspers, 1982; Gudykunst and Hammer, 1989). In recent years, Gallois, Franklyn-Stokes, Giles, and Coupland (1988) postulated a theory of communication accommodation based on the previous works of Howard Giles. This theoretical framework embraces the idea that varying degrees of in-group dependency and out-group affiliation cause individual patterned behaviors, which change contextually. Giles, Bourhis and Taylor (1977) introduced the concept of group vitality, alternatively known as ethnolinguistic vitality. The authors contend that this influences the degree to which group members behave as a group in the presence of out-group members. The extent of the group's vitality is directly proportionate to its ability to survive in multilingual settings. Naturally, this places identity and group membership in a sociolinguistic framework. Status, demographics, and institutional support were the three factors identified by the authors that affect vitality. It has been discovered that groups with less vitality will linguistically assimilate (Sachdev, Bourhis, Phang, and D'Eye, 1987). Assimilation has always been a factor in identity studies. The study of cultural, racial, and ethnic identity has been no different.

Anthropologists Kroeber and Kluckhohn announced in 1952 that culture, race, and ethnicity had often been confused as interchangeable terms to describe groups who share a common set of characteristics. The actual studies delineated relatively specific characteristics and hence destroyed much of the commonality of these descriptors. Gordon Allport (1954), even in reprinted editions of *The Nature of Prejudice*, explained that race relates to biological as well as hereditary ties, while ethnicity indicates social and cultural ties. Collier and Thomas's cultural identity theory (1988) recognized the distinction between these terms and decided that culture is one of many identities expressed in communication encounters. The authors further recommended that cultural identity not be treated as an independent variable in intercultural research, since there is more than one identity at work in any circumstance.

Racial identity is prominently studied in psychology and has been considered among communication scholars (along with class and religion) to be a type of ethnic identity. Ethnic identity is broadly defined according to symbols and meanings employed by group members who have had sustained contact over an extensive period of time. Their memberships are either ascribed or avowed. Ascribed (or imposed) membership is a well-known sociological appellate used to suggest a membership in a group whose ties are unavoidable such as a racial group. Avowed identities are self-selected, such as those related to a language or religion. It is only when a communicator's ascribed identity is consistent with his or her partner's avowed identity that intercultural competence is at its greatest (Collier and Thomas, 1988; Collier and Thomas, 1989; Gudykunst and Nishida, 1989; Hecht, Collier, and Ribeau, 1993). In other words, when a communicator's behavior is similar to the enacted behavior of a second communicator, then intercultural competence is said to be at an optimal level, since the two interactants share a common sense of what is normal, effective, and appropriate. Hecht, Collier, and Ribeau (1993) present their communication theory of ethnic identity as a direct link to intercultural communication competence. They assert that ethnic identity be defined as

a perceived membership in an ethnic culture that is enacted in the appropriate and effective use of symbols and cultural narratives, similar interpretations and meanings, and common ancestry and traditions. *Identity* [italics added] implies a sense of self or personhood and ethnic identity is the subjective sense of belonging to or membership in an ethnic culture. (p. 30)

CHAPTER SNAPSHOT

The sociological, psychological, and communication perspectives vary in their approaches of the study of identity, but undeniably identity is an issue that cannot be ignored within any of these disciplines. Its prevalence across disciplinary studies and its regard for the creation and maintenance of human relationships is paramount to human survival. Du Bois's (1903) double-consciousness is a term really meant to capture the frustration resulting from this constant vacillation from one identity mode to another (i.e., Cultural Identity Negotiation). It is an explanation of a coping strategy implemented to reduce racial tension that has emanated from racial prejudice and accommodation.

Chapter 3

Origins: A Foundation for the Discussion of Race in America

CONCEPTUAL BEGINNINGS: RACE, ETHNICITY, AND CULTURE

The issues of race, race relations, and racial stratification within social scientific research have been critical to the development of the terms "ethnicity" and "culture." Before discussing racial, ethnic, and cultural identity, it is vital that an historical framework is presented. The emergence of race, ethnicity, and culture as identity referents has an extensive history and significant linkage to sociological, psychological, and communication theory. Central to this brief overview are two interpretations of race (biological and sociological), followed by contemporary definitions of race, ethnicity, and culture.

Biological Considerations of Race

Yehudi Webster (1992), in his comprehensive overview of racial theory, clearly states that there has been more than one attempt to specify the origin of the term "race"; however, this issue has yet to be resolved. Nonetheless, most scholars do agree that naturalists, zoologists, anthropologists, and biologists are the progenitors of early racial theory. Cornel West (1993) reveals that the term racc is derived from the French doctor Francois Bernier, who in 1684, devised it as a nomenclature for classifying human bodies primarily according to skin color.

In the first edition of *Systema Naturae* written in 1735, Carl von Linnaeus (1964, p. 34) taxonomized six human races according to skin color, geographical location, and civilization. The "homo-Europeus" was described as especially gifted with intellectual abilities superior to other homo sapiens. This commentary was typical among eighteenth-century natural scientists and should be recognized as an initial contribution toward racial division and scientific analysis of human subjects. These classifications created the foundation for modern presentations of African Americans throughout the disciplines. The formation of this body places the "white race at the center of history," with a conscious exclusion of other races' contributions (Webster,

1992). Stephen Gould (1981) provided further evidence of this in discussing the ideas of Georges Cuvier, a preeminent scientist whose ideas were well respected, he having founded the scientific disciplines of geology, paleontology, and comparative astronomy. Cuvier denounced the human potential of African natives, declaring them "the most degraded of human races, whose form approaches that of a beast and whose intelligence is nowhere great enough to arrive at regular government" (p. 36). Gould (1981) also mentioned philosopher David Hume, who was recognized as a polygenist, one who believes that not all humans share a common birthplace. This multiple-origins theory [i.e., polygeny] facilitated the argument that Blacks were inferior, while debunking the dominant-recessive genes argument which proves Africa to be the only birthplace of humankind (Welsing, 1991).

Hume, in 1766, supported the Negro inferiority hypothesis and argued that no other race is more accomplished, honorable, intelligent, or energetic than whites. Johann Blumenbach (1825) considered the same three characteristics as Linnaeus in his categorization of five races, calling whites the optimal human species. Early evidence of a systematized formulation of race superiority is found in nineteenth-century anthropologist Arthur de Gobineau's (1853/1967) four-volume work entitled *The Inequality of Human Races*. Caucasoid, Mongoloid, and Negroid are the three typologies presented in this influential manuscript, with the Negroid race occupying the lowest end of the Gobineau ladder:

The Negroid variety is the lowest, and stands at the foot of the ladder. The animal character, that appears in the shape of the pelvis, is stamped on the Negro from birth, and foreshadows his destiny. . . . We come now to the white peoples. These are gifted with reflective energy, or rather with an energetic intelligence. When they are cruel, they are conscious of their cruelty; it is very doubtful whether such a consciousness exists in the Negro. The principle motive is honor. . . . [This] is unknown to both the yellow and the black man (Gobineau,1853/1967, p. 206).

Franz Boas, a leading critic of biological-deterministic conceptions of race in the 1890s, launched an assault marked by the phrase "supraindividual organic identity." This pertained to an heirarchial and categorical arrangement of human personalities based on bio-physical characteristics (Montagu, 1974). Yet in sharp contrast, Hegel's (1899/1956) *Philosophy of History* indicated that without the White man, Black people would have no culture, (which helps explain the seeming inability to define Blackness without reference to a juxtaposed Whiteness.)

Scholars like Gobineau (1853/1967), who supported racial categorization, further differentiated the white, yellow, and black peoples by identifying Aryan Nordics as the superior set of whites, as opposed to those with a southern or eastern European lineage. Staples (1987) noted that eastern and southern Europeans in the twentieth century have been assigned as second-world cultures, while western and northern Europeans maintain a first-world status. This initiated the suggestion of an existing white ethnic group, composed of such "ethnics" as Jews, Poles, Italians, and Irish (Webster, 1992). Another predominant reason for the division of whites is that some European descendants were believed to have little regard for maintaining the purity of white blood; there was a fear of any possibility for cross-breeding or genetic annihilation.

Kelves (1985) asserted that eugenics provides scientific support that Whites with superior stock produce intellectually superior children. When racial mixing occurs, the consequence is a degraded race. Eugenics, "the science of improving a breed or species, especially the human race, by careful selection of parents," became a primary concern for the Aryan Nordics (Woolf, 1977, p. 394). Frances Cress Welsing (1991) addresses this phobia in her book *The Isis Papers: The Keys to the Colors.* Welsing captures the essence of this justifiable discomfort by stating that color always annihilates the non-color, white, both phenotypically and genetically.

Following the primitive race hypotheses of the seventeenth, eighteenth, and nineteenth centuries, several publications emerged that critically assessed the history, development, and usage of race across disciplines (Banton, 1983; Conrad, 1966; De Tocqueville, 1832/1956; Gossett, 1965; Montagu, 1945; Myrdal, 1944; Omi and Winant, 1986; Park, 1950). The idea of race as being solely biological and a determining factor of intellect began to dissipate around the 1930s, and the political, social, economic, and psychological dimensions began to emerge in race-related scientific research (Montagu, 1974).

Sociological Considerations of Race

After having classified race as a biologically related characteristic, scientists began examining the differences in meaning-creation among the classified groups. The initial labels, "Christian" and "English" used to describe European settlers, were replaced with "White" around 1680, and it was an applicable term until White immigrants of diverse backgrounds and lineages entered the United States in the 1700s (Omi and Winant, 1986). These new Whites were classified as ethnic groups, which divided American Whites as a result. Andrew Hacker (1992) explains that in the 1830s Alexis De Tocqueville, a Frenchman who traveled in the United States, named his hosts "Anglo-Americans," because the majority of them claimed British ancestry. Since this designation has been proposed, the influx of White ethnic groups has made this term a misnomer with respect to the entire American populace. However, Hacker indicates that Americans are reverting to de Tocqueville's original characterization of the White population; there is not as much emphasis on distinguishing one group of Whites from others.

Banton (1983) suggested that the initial conceptions of race indicated its permanence and relationship to lineage differences via physical, intellectual, and behavioral characteristics. The research of polygenist Samuel George Horton was mentioned by Gould (1981), who reported that Morton collected eight-hundred crania from various parts of the world, measured their respective weights, and discovered a link between cranial weight and capacity for intelligence. European descendants had an average cranial capacity of ninety-six cubic inches, while Negro skulls had an average capacity of eighty-three cubic inches, thus giving evidence of superiority. This area of study became known as craniometry.

Webster (1992) posits that the naturalists, biologists, and anthropologists had an additional role as sociologists, examining group memberships and roles. Race was not related simply to skin color, nose size, and hair texture, but also to nation, civilization and culture. The behavioral implications that accompanied a civilized condition or cultural arrangement added depth to scientific examinations of race. However, as the field of sociology expanded, race was no longer an operable term for describing physical, social, and cultural attributes. The paradigm shift (Kuhn, 1970) included the introduction of a new term "ethnicity." The emergence of this new term was very slow and gradual.

A pivotal point in the evolution was the establishment of racial theory. According to Yehudi Webster (1992), there were three major areas of confusion that affected the maturity of this newly conceived theory: there were disagreements regarding the number and characteristics of human races, the presence of pure races and their origin, and the relationship of race to such personality traits as intelligence.   Carl Hirsch (1972) indicated that some scientists listed only three races, while others list as many as three hundred. Common enumerations were five, six, nine, and thirty. He noted that several anthropologists had eliminated the term from their studies because of its inherent ambiguities.   Some biologists had done likewise and further claimed that physical distinctions can be so varied that there are no races. According to Diamond and Belasco (1980), early social theorists created a conceptual link between biology and behavior, and committed themselves to viewing race as a social construct.

Anatomical differences and racial causation were the centerpiece of racial theoretical analysis. Charles Darwin's (1859) *Origin of the Species* was one of the first works under the rubric of racial theory. He was a monogenist, one who believes that humans share a common origin, but he still relegated blacks to the lowest level on the human continuum. He attributed their enslavement to their position in the chain of being. Winthrop Jordan (1968), in *White Over Black,* submitted that slavery continued in post-Revolutionary America due to the assessments by whites that the Negro should maintain his divinely designated and rightful place in the natural order -- the bottom of the chain of being. By the latter part of the eighteenth century, the Great Chain of Being was very popular, commonly referred to as "the chain," "the scale of beings" or "one's rank in creation" (Lovejoy, 1960, p. 13). The "chain" is said to date back to the days of Aristotle, but it was later developed by seventeenth century philosopher Gottfried Wilhelm von Liebniz. Racial theory persisted due to its primary function of preserving the superiority of whites. Omi and Winant claim that racial theory is formed by existing race relations. "Within any given historical period, a particular racial theory is dominant" (p. 11).

The impact that this had on minorities was later examined in the psychology and sociology disciplines (Burkitt, 1992; Goffman, 1959; 1961; Omi and Winant, 1986; Staples, 1987; Webster, 1992; Welsing, 1991; Wilson, 1990,1993). Webster identifies a school of general racial theorists composed of individuals such as Carl von Linnaeus, Arthur de Gobineau, Lothrop Stoddard, and Madison Grant.   Sociologists fully invested in racial theory, as it came to be conceptualized as an interconnected network of behavior, social inequality, and social control. This announced the beginning of research on race relations, racial-cultural contact, confrontation, and victimization. In the 1920s, Robert Park and colleagues from the University of Chicago initiated a subdiscipline -- sociology of race relations. These scientists became known as the Chicago School (Omi and Winant, 1986). They were certain that biological considerations of race were not going to be eradicated immediately, yet it was understood that a sociologist's work needed to be centered around intergroup relations and the attached social meaning (Stebbins, 1992). Hence, there was the advent of "ethnicity" as a theoretic label to describe a peculiar type of social group membership (Glazer and Moynihan, 1975). The work of the Chicago School preempted Gunnar Myrdal's (1944) *An American Dilemma,* Gordon Allport's (1954) *Nature of Prejudice,* and Yehuda Amir's (1969) work on contact hypothesis.

Allport (1954) discussed the differences in the terms *race* and *ethnicity,* and admits the ambivalence created by their use. He quoted Clyde Kluckhohn (1961) as having stated, "Though the concept of race is genuine enough, there is perhaps no field of science in which the misunderstandings among educated people are so frequent and so serious" (p. 107). Allport defined race as that which pertains to hereditary ties, and ethnicity as relating to social and cultural ties. To illustrate the difficulty in differentiating terms, Allport explained how Jews are classified. The author indicated that 70 percent of Jews live in Russia, Israel, and the United States, and that they share a social history that is bound by a religious commitment to Judaism. However, this group has such strong social ties, that it is often mistaken for a culture. The remarkable physiological variances from one Jew to the next belies the notion that Jews are a race. It is the religious and linguistic commonalities that ensure the ethnic identity of this group of individuals. The only exception is those who individuals who are indigenous citizens of or ancestrally tied to Jerusalem, in which case they are Jews by culture.

All the aforementioned works are classics in race relations studies and have provided the transition from a sole concentration on race relations to distributed studies on ethnic group relations.

Even since the 1950s, however, both terms have been used within sociological studies. Robert Park (1950) contended that race has always been a social construct, since individuals not only create social meaning but also assume behavior and personality traits based on observed biological features. Park admitted that the debate on whether race is primarily biological or social is virtually endless, but he maintained that categories mean nothing without correlative meaning.

Culture has been loosely depicted as a civilized set of values, beliefs, and folk traditions within sociological studies (Stebbins, 1992). Montagu (1962) observed that cultural anthropologists believe they are studying the same phenomenon, but that some define culture as "learned behavior" and others suppose it is an "abstraction of behavior" (p. 38). Cultural anthropologist E.B. Tylor's (1871/1889) definition of culture has been recognized as the first documented explanation within anthropological and sociological research (Webster, 1992): "Culture . . . is that complex whole which includes knowledge, belief, art, morals, law and customs, and any other capabilities and habits acquired by man as a member of society" (Tylor, 1871/1889, p. 3). It was quickly understood that culture implied something *shared* by more than one person. Sociological studies have focused on ethnic group memberships and societally based values, with reference to both race and culture.

Psychological studies have primarily concentrated on race and culture. Recent communication studies, however, accentuate culture with some reference to race and ethnicity (Chen and Starosta, 1998; Hecht, Collier, and Ribeau, 1993; Hecht, Ribeau, and Alberts, 1989; Kim and Sharkey, 1995; Martin, Hecht, and Larkey, 1994; Pajaczkowska and Young, 1992; Ting-Toomey, 1989).

Historically, race has been instituted within the language of most disciplines. In tracing the history of sociology, psychology, and communication, race was the predominant term used to describe what is now distinguished as ethnicity or culture. For example, Andrea Rich (1974), a communication scholar and author of *Interracial Communication,* devoted an entire book to the examination of race, racial stereotypes, racial prejudice, and interethnic hostility discovered in communication patterns among Blacks and Whites. Race was described as physical, social, and psychological. Rich explained that culture is "the sum total of the learned behaviors of a group of people" (p. 5). Contraculture, however, is the imposition of one race over another. Interethnic communication is defined as "communication between members of various non-White groups who have shared the experience of being a racial minority in a White-dominated structure" (p. 13). While race is the primary theme, it is clear that works like this one augmented the paradigm shift from race to culture as a preferred descriptor of groups such as African Americans and European Americans.

Ethnicity is a group construct, and it is rarely used to describe the individual-oriented study of the human mind within psychology. Culture is more clearly understood and defined by anthropologists as a collage of communication patterns, values, beliefs, practices, mores, myths, legends, heroes, culinary interests, and religious affiliations (Hall, 1959; Kluckhohn and Strodtbeck, 1961; Kroeber and Kluckhohn, 1952; Montagu, 1945; Tylor, 1871/1889). Race is often used to refer to a group of people that are classified according to nationality, common physical characteristics, and shared ancestry (Allport, 1954; Gossett, 1965; Myrdal, 1944; Omi and Winant, 1986; Rich, 1974;). Culture is most often equated with worldview (Ani, 1994; X et al., 1975). At the inception of the communication discipline, studies were primarily concerned with issues of interracial and intraracial communication, although Edward T. Hall (1959) first mentioned intercultural communication in his book *The Silent Language.* As the discipline has matured, so has its understanding of culture. Presently, more research is concerned with issues of culture than ever before. Race is becoming a virtually outdated concept within intercultural communication. Yet, its historical significance is still understood and appreciated. Practically speaking, many public and private industry organizations still use the words race and ethnicity on employment applications and other important documents; hence the terms cannot be avoided by either academicians or those in other professions. However, the meaning of each term needs to be critically defined across the disciplines to ensure that scholars are really studying the same phenomena.

DEFINITIONS OF RACE, ETHNICITY, AND CULTURE

In the middle of 1997, President Clinton launched the dialogue on race. This was an unprecedented event in the history of the United States. This is not to say that the US has never explored ways to "deal with" the problem of race in America, rather that the US has historically presented insufficient resolutions to a very severe social disease -- racism. Despite efforts ranging from Reconstruction to Gunnar Myrdal's "melting pot theory," racial, economic, social, and political inequality persists in the US. So, it is unique that a "dialogue on race" has been initiated, but the dialogue will go nowhere unless those who participate in the conversation understand what race really means. Therefore, race, ethnicity, and culture must be defined critically. According to Robert Stebbins (1992), "Strictly speaking, from the standpoint of biological science, 'races' do not exist. As we shall see, there is no biological basis for the concept of race. . . . The commonsense idea of race is based on inherited physical similarities" (p. 22). While there is much debate about this, it should be made clear that race is a biological construct that has social meaning; consequently, it could be argued that race is both biological and social. Stebbins's (1992) primary contention that "races" do not exist is supported by sociologists but rejected by biologists, who claim that physical differences are widely varied within and among races; the tremendous disparity among scientists regarding the existence, number, and types of races supports this claim.

Race and culture are not the same. Yehudi Webster (1992) claims that race is the product of anatomical differences. The author rejects the alignment of race with culture and proposes that scholars not consider each race as having its own culture, lest he/she submits to a loose interpretation of culture. Even if culture is described as the composite of shared symbols, beliefs, ideas, and values, there must be some characteristic that distinguishes it from race and ethnicity. Ethnicity is often thought to be related to groups that are not White Anglo-Saxon Protestant; however, several publications contend that there is a White ethnic population consisting of Irish, Polish, Italian, German, and Mediterranean peoples (Fellows, 1972; Hraba, 1979; Lieberson, 1985; Ryan, 1973; Weber, 1961). These scholars explain that there has been some debate as to whether these groups can even be called "White." Whiteness has become such an all-encompassing term. As you will read in Chapter 7, being White is often considered synonymous with what it means to be American. This sets up an I-Other dichotomy between White Americans and "other" Americans -- a relationship that leads to several forms of exclusion, including but not limited to socioeconomic imparity. Nonetheless, ethnicity is not a term reserved for non-Whites.

The etymology of the word "ethnic" traces to the Greek *ethnikos*, meaning a foreign group or nationality within a society. Also, the Latin *ethnicus* not only meant foreigner, but also "heathen." Stebbins (1992) maintains that present conceptions of the word "ethnic" are understood similarly. While he recognizes that White ethnic groups exist, he claims that ethnic group references are most often tied to groups considered to be non-White, foreign, and heathen. Asante (1990) also expounds on the description of ethnic groups as displaced peoples, referring to ethnomusicology and ethnomethodology and noting that Eurocentric writers omitted Europeans from their studies, suggesting that ethno-research included only non-Europeans. Minority status, according to Stebbins, is attained after having been victimized by white supremacy and "assigned" to secondary or tertiary status as an American citizen. Among the ethnic groups who share minority status in America are "Blacks, Irish, Italians, Germans, Chinese, Mexicans, French Canadians, Amerindians, and East Asians" (p. 404). Blacks are the only group mentioned that lacks a land-referent within the group name. Abrahams (1970) argues that any critical definition of culture must include a connection to a land mass that represents the origin of the culture. The omission of a land-referent facilitates the argument that Blacks have no culture or cultural identity (Levine, 1977). In the 1980s, this basic logic was revealed to Jesse Jackson, and he called for, among all Americans, a national shift in cultural identifiers -- from "Black" to "African American." It has often confused outsiders who don't really know what to call the once-named "Blacks." It has also prompted discussion around political correctness and diversity initiatives in other communities.

Meanwhile, another similar discussion has been going on in regard to "unhyphenated Whites." Lieberson (1985) coined this term to imply a cultural displacement of some Whites in America. In his writings, he clearly recognizes the dilemma created by labeling all other groups ethnicities and not quite knowing what it means to be White. Lieberson describes the lack of hyphenated cultural labels among "Whites" as a tribute to multiculturalism. He contends that many Americans are products of different-race parents, consequently the purity of White blood is virtually dissolved, forcing White Americans either to come to terms with their own multicultural heritage, or dismiss their mixed cultural lineage and generically define themselves as "White." The rationale often given for the "whiteness as [an] absent center" motif is that identities change over time, thus it is unimportant to commit oneself to a cultural identity -- an amenity that potentially prevents negotiation of cultural identity (Pajaczkowska and Young, 1992, p. 58).

So then, how do we come to understand ethnicity? Ethnicity is often thought to be socially-defined and constructed on the basis of cultural criteria (Jones, 1991). Hraba (1979, p. 27) provided the best definition of ethnic groups, as "self-conscious collectivities of people, who on the basis of a common origin or a separate subculture, maintain a distinction between themselves and outsiders." The subculture that Hraba (1979) mentioned poses some sense of ambiguity, as it is often cited to mean religion, language, nationality, or culinary interests (Fellows, 1972; Montagu, 1945; Weber, 1961; Webster, 1992). Yet, it is generally agreed upon that race is subsumed under the category of ethnicity, and ethnicity is a subdivision of culture.

Culture was first defined in print by E.B. Tylor (1871/1889, 2nd ed., p. 3), who stated, "Culture or civilization, taken in its wide ethnographic sense is that complex whole, which includes knowledge, beliefs, art, law, morals, customs, and any other capabilities and habits acquired by [wo]man as a member of society." Edward T. Hall (1959) criticized this definition, pointing out its "lack of rigorous specificity" (p. 20). Hall responded to this void with an entire theory on culture, composed of ten elements called the Primary Message System (PMS), supported by three message components (sets, isolates, and patterns). The theory was described as bio-basic and infra-cultural, exhibiting a strong linkage between culture and communication. A less intricate but suitable conception of culture is found in Clifford Geertz's (1973, p. 12) *The*

Interpretation of Cultures.   Culture was defined within the text as "an historically transmitted pattern of meanings embodied in symbols, a system of inherited conceptions expressed in symbolic forms by means of which men [and women] communicate, perpetuate, and develop their knowledge about and attitudes toward life." This definition is important, since it accounts for the evolutionary quality of culture, the process and pattern-based structure of culture, and the traditional /cross-generational transmission of culture. Moreover, the definition relates culture to symbol sharing and interpretations of reality. The only missing, but often assumed, component is the tie to a geographical location. Culture, according to Marshall Singer (1987), must be viewed perceptually and therefore instituted and incorporated by an identity group into their "everyday lives." Geertz (1973) submitted that culture has been ill defined and diluted due to a plethora of definitions. Considering the common misunderstanding of the distinctions between race, ethnicity and culture, I would quickly agree with him. Culture is often used to describe subcultural groups such as those related to gender, age, physical impairment, sexual preference, language, nationality, and religion. In fact, any set of people are thought to have their own culture as long as they are united for some expressed purpose. For example, culture has been used to describe hip-hop music lovers, as well as public and private industry organizations.

As a result of the confusion, it became necessary for me to devise my own definition, which clarified some of the overlaps. Culture is a term used here to describe a set of patterns, beliefs, behaviors, institutions, symbols and practices shared and perpetuated by a consolidated group of individuals connected by an ancestral heritage and a concomitant geographical reference location (Ani, 1994; Diop, 1991; Holloway, 1990; Levine, 1977; Nobles, 1986).

Biological and sociological considerations of race have proposed disparate conceptions of race, ethnicity, and culture.   It is the attempt of this investigation to expose a pattern of conceptual development by critically examining the history of these terms within the social scientific, psychological, and communication disciplines. It is important to note that race and ethnicity are still preferred terms in social scientific research. Race and culture are preferred in the field of psychology. Within communication, however, culture is increasingly becoming the preferred term; ethnicity and race are still employed, but to a diminishing degree.

CHAPTER SNAPSHOT

This chapter provides a cursory purview of the literature concerning the conceptual beginnings of race, ethnicity, and culture. These terms have often been ambiguous in identity research. So, I wanted to offer some clarity by providing an explanation of biological and sociological considerations of races, as well as contemporary definitions of race, ethnicity, and culture.   As Kluckhohn suggests these three terms, while seemingly rather simple are very complex and very often misunderstood. Certainly, much of the recent literature by interdisciplinary scholars, such as that of Margaret Anderson and Patricia Hill-Collins, Paula Rothenberg, Paulo Friere, Cornel West, bell hooks, Janet Helms, Wade Nobles, Marimba Ani, Ruth Frankenberg, Bjorn Krondorfer,

Molefi Asante, Brenda J. Allen, Melbourne Cummings, Marsha Houston, Bill Gudykunst, Bill Starosta, Al Gonzalez, Victoria Chen, Celeste Condit and Michael Hecht provide us with increasing clarity as to the denotative and connotative meanings of these terms. There is still room for more research from different disciplinary, methodological, and conceptual perspectives.

Chapter 4

Racial, Ethnic and Cultural Identities: An Interdisciplinary Perspective

Very little identity research has critically examined the significance of the terms -- "race," "ethnicity," and "culture"; therefore the following three reviews concerning these identity prefixes will include literature that assumes the reader will conceptually link race with something more than biological characteristics. The studies included under the heading "race and identity" are ones that mostly discuss race from a nomothetic orientation. Those included under "ethnicity and identity" either discuss ethnicity extensively or explain the study from a socially defined or group-oriented perspective, emphasizing a subcultural element, such as language. The "culture and identity" section comprises research related to several issues including, but not limited to, worldview cultural variability, and a patterned behavior within and among multiple groups.

RACE AND IDENTITY

Psychology

As previously mentioned, race has historically been defined in America to signify the inherent superiority of Whites over non-Whites. Consequently, early psychological research on race concerned itself with "inherent" personality differences between White and non-White peoples. The preferred terminology eventually became the "majority" in relationship to "minority" groups (Stebbins, 1992). Moreover, several initial psychological researchers performed comparative analyses of intellectual ability and behavioral causality (Binet and Simon, 1911; Goddard, 1914; Goddard, 1919; Stoddard, 1920). In fact, in 1912 a German psychologist, W. Stern, created the intelligence quotient, better known as I.Q. The results of the aforementioned research always confirmed the White superiority hypothesis. Gould (1981) explained that craniometry, for example, became a serious venture for these early psychologists. Heads were measured by weight and length in order to discover brain capacity. It was believed that those with larger brains were more intelligent. Eventually, this practice was abandoned and replaced with interest in racial identity, personality, and attitudes.   The original research examined only   Black and White respondents, usually school-aged children (Boynton, 1941; Clark and Clark, 1947; T. E. Davis, 1937).   Davis (1937) and Boynton's (1941) studies found that minorities, who had been castigated by the dominant group tended to express similar oppressive attitudes within their own groups.   This type of research supported the continual development of the race relations research instituted by Robert Parks.

Kenneth and Mamie Clark conducted their monumental research study in order to gather evidence regarding racial self-conceptions of elementary children. This is one of the clearest examples of initial racial identity research in the field of psychology.   The husband-wife team found that about three-fourths of the respondents were able to distinguish between White and Colored by the age of three, and almost all of the subjects could identify the differences by the age of seven.   Race was discovered to be the principal factor impacting self-identification among Black school children.   The investigation involved a response to four requests, among other measuring techniques. The four requests were as follows: Give me the doll you like to play with, or the doll you like best; Give me the doll that is the nice doll; Give me the doll that looks bad; give me the doll that is the nice color. The majority of the three-to-seven-year-old children chose the white doll over the brown doll after each favorable request.

White and Parham (1990) rejected the self-hatred thesis proposed by Clark and Clark's research, however this type of literature continued in psychological publications throughout the 1950s, with such works as Kardiner and Ovessey's (1951) *Mark of Oppression.*   These scholars, like several others (Baldwin, 1980; Baldwin, Brown, and Hopkins, 1991; Helm, 1990), contend that the self-hatred thesis assumes a psychological obligation to mimic white behavior. While Amos Wilson (1978), a renowned child psychologist, did recognize Clark and Clark's (1947) study as being outdated, he valued its precocious forecast of his own notion of "schizmic" versus "restricted" living (p.80). Schizmic living is described as a predisposition to be a member of the Black middle class in America, and being forced to live a schizoid existence of either White or Black identity. Restrictive living reflects the denied access to socioeconomic resources primarily experienced by those with a lower class status. Wilson presumed that the "negotiation" is not as much of a necessity for the lower class. Hare (1991) concurs with Wilson's assessment of the Black middle class and further posits that these "Black Anglo-Saxons" have undergone a metamorphosis over time:

Whereas 1960's Black Anglo-Saxons had focused on simple mimicry of white characteristics -- and Black Anglo-Saxons in the 1970's and early 1980's endeavored to incorporate the very physiognomy of white people, or portions of white people --   Black Anglo-Saxons in the late 1980's and the year 1990 conspicuously incorporated the worldview and sociopolitical thinking of white people (Hare, 1991, p. ii).

In regards to this "psychoexistential complex," Frantz Fanon laments, "However painful it may be for me to accept this conclusion, I am obliged to state it: For the Black man there is only one destiny, and it is white" (p. 17). This prognosis was refuted by Vernon Dixon (1976), who claimed the possibility of a diunital approach to identity management. By first introducing the "either/or approach," Dixon illustrated the significance of a synthetic conceptualization of Black identity, combining Black and White identity to achieve ultimate harmony. Dixon stated:

Accordingly, the real conflict, most likely occurring subconsciously in Black people, is that on the one hand, they have a sense of embodying two radically different identities, one White American, one African-oriented (Black); on the other, they have a sense of not embodying these same two identities. How do Black people resolve this conflict? Do they deny both these identities, assert affinity with both, or assert affinity with one and deny the other? (pp. 33-34)

Dixon sought to resolve the ontological conundrum by proposing a cultural diunity theory. He offered a both/and versus an either/or conception of identity. Ideally, neither identity is denied, both coexist harmoniously, recognizing the authenticity of the other. Mutual recognition of the other, Fanon asserts, is the human enactment of the Hegelian dialectic, which affirms human existence.

Samaj (1981) offered a three-tiered model of extended identity placed on a continuum with Afro-centric and Eurocentric polarities. The three tiers consist of the alien, diffused, and collective identities. The aliens do not endorse a collective consciousness. Instead they isolate themselves from the collective and function independently as individuals. The diffused seek to balance a collective mentality with an individualist orientation. The collectives are those who identify with an African-centered perspective of interconnectedness with the masses. White and Parham (1990) celebrate Samaj's work and explain that its primary utility is as an heuristic catalyst. Because it fails to account for any psychological growth through setting fixed identity categories, it encourages future research that will concern itself with a process-oriented conception of identity.

The concealment of identity as well as its multiple forms have been a major concern for Black psychologists for decades and continue to be a priority on many psychological researchers' agendas.

Sociology

Du Bois (1903), considered a sociologist by many scholars, accurately predicted that the color line would be the major obstacle to race relations in the twentieth century (Allport, 1954; Amir, 1969; Hacker, 1992; Myrdal, 1944; Omi and Winant, 1986; Stoddard, 1920). Gunnar Myrdal's classic *The American Dilemma* reported findings suggesting that Blacks would be fully assimilated into the mainstream after committing themselves to an amalgamated climate of cultural control -- the melting pot. Myrdal challenged the American people to unite as one culture, the American culture, essentially to assimilate. While such Black intellectuals as Countee Cullen and Sterling Brown served as assistants on the Myrdal project, the results indicated an unfavorable resolution. At the time, this sounded like a second Reconstruction, and was welcomed by Blacks. A decade later, however, Allport (1954) announced that race relations had been unaltered and that racial prejudice persisted as normal. Racial conflict was quite apparent, as the number of sit-ins and protests increased. Government officials, organizational leaders, and academicians began to devise methods of reducing racial tension (Silberman, 1964). By the latter part of the 1960s, Yehudi Amir (1969) had developed the contact hypothesis, which stated that ethnic prejudice was inversely proportionate to the extent of ethnic group contact. In other words, racial tension could theoretically be reduced if the ethnic groups were more exposed to one another. It was already clear that a major barrier to cross-cultural interaction was the anxiety produced by the unexpected (Oberg, 1960). Stephan and Stephan (1992) provide a modern analysis of this phenomenon, advancing the work of Amir (1969) by forwarding a theory of intergroup anxiety. A reduction in intergroup anxiety was believed to be directly related to an improved climate of racial harmony. Meanwhile, decade after decade, the Kerner Commission on Civil Disorders, instituted in the 1960s, reported that "Blacks and Whites are moving toward two societies, one Black, one White, separate, hostile, and unequal" (Hacker, 1992, p. 7). Several writers referred to this schism as the "two Americas" (Fager, 1967; Silberman, 1964; Staples, 1987). Fager (1967) indicated that both races have lived in the same social, cultural, political and economic milieu but maintain contradictory experiences. Fager assigns as the reason for this disparity a difference between a prosperous worldview and a slave worldview. Blacks, who perforce occupy the slave worldview, struggle with a sense of inferiority. Robert Staples captures the substance of what Fager unsuccessfully attempts to explain, asserting that colonial society has produced a racial hierarchy with Whites in the domineering position: "The culturally distinct racial minority finds itself being judged by how close it conforms to Anglo-Saxon norms" (p. 13). He further notes that a major paradigm shift in race relations studies has been the study of racial domination itself. Whether one speaks of "minorities" (Stebbins, 1992) or the "fourth world" (Staples, 1987), racial groups sustain intergroup conflict as a consequence of hegemonic rule (Gramsci, 1983).

Minorities continue to avoid what Patricia Hill Collins (1990) labels the "matrix of domination," while struggling to maintain a sense of self between identity shifts (Ani, 1994; Fanon, 1967; Hare, 1991). Friederes and Goldenberg (1982) endorsed the coordination of multiple identities as opposed to a singular self-concept. This coping strategy is considered to be both flexible and mobile. These authors warn that identity salience should be contextually defined, and that sub-identities such as linguistic or religious identities should not be ignored. Parenti (1969) wrote that complementary identifications are created throughout life; therefore identity is a process, not a stage. The debate concerning the maintenance of identity, whether singular or multiple, continues, while the emphasis shifts to using both terms, race and ethnicity, to describe one's concept of a socially motivated identity.

Communication

Certainly, there are multiple identities (Chen and Starosta, 1998) and communication scholars have explored how they can be understood from a contracultural perspective. "Contraculture" was defined by Andrea Rich (1974) in her book *Interracial Communication* as that which occurs as a result of an "imposition of one culture on another" (p. 9). Rich recommended that intercultural and interracial relationships be appreciated within the context of intervening variables, such as power and language. In addition, she charged Whites with the creation of racist language embedded with divisive cues. The example she used was the terms "Black" and "White," and their inherent polar opposition. "As a cultural phenomenon, language of course, is learned," Rich explained, "It is culturally induced and developed, and as such, reflects the values of the culture. Language enculturates the individual by predetermining how [s/]he sees the world" (p. 130). The author also attributed race prejudice toward Blacks as the instigator of assimilation and socialization. This is followed by role playing and the development of a counterculture or subculture. The counterculture is defined as a representation of the norms and values of the established dominant group at the expense of abandoning one's primary culture. Burke and Tully (1977) added another dynamic to this notion of counterculture by suggesting co-identities and counter-identities. "Co-identities" are the manifested form of an individual's multiple roles and identities, such as those related to age, physical impairment, or sexual preference. "Counter-identities" are enacted roles that augment asymmetrical relationships, such as parent/child or supervisor/subordinate relationships.

Racial identity in communication research has traditionally accentuated racial imparity, interracial interaction, and accommodation. Giles, Coupland, and Coupland (1991) conducted research on sociolinguistic accommodation, and address issues related to excessive concession of linguistic identity. This was termed "overaccommodation" and was pejoratively received as patronizing behavior. Kochman's (1981) ethnographic studies reveal that the communication patterns of Blacks and Whites are dissimilar, and that therefore behavioral interpretations of each interaction episode can potentially become problematic. The principal reason for racial tension and infringement on Black identity, Kochman admits, is that "Whites assume they are operating according to identical speech and cultural conventions. . . This assumption . . . speaks to the general public failure to recognize that Black norms and conventions in these areas differ from those of Whites." The verbal and nonverbal communication among the two racial groups is quite distinctive. Asante (1978) posits that a convergence of situational and cultural modalities is key to a successful and effective relationship between the races. This notion of situational sensitivity and cultural awareness is endorsed by Dickens and Dickens (1992), who claim that workplace organizations are experiencing decreased morale and productivity due not utilizing their full human resource potential. Asante's (1990) establishment of situation, culture, and interaction as primary units of analysis has led to an improved appreciation of effective interracial communication. Since the late 1980s, identity has become a much more pervasive issue among intercultural communication scholars. In the 1990s, there is very little mention of interracial communication. It was formerly the name of a communication subdiscipline, which is presently known as intercultural communication. This shift provided a pivotal point in communication research and encouraged a critical examination of the terms race and culture (Pajaczkowska and Young, 1992). Rattansi (1992) encourages a "critical re-reading of culture . . . [since] 'race' and identity are inherently contestable social and political categories" (p. 141).

ETHNICITY AND IDENTITY

Psychology

White and Parham (1990) endorse multicultural models of psychology in *Psychology of Blacks,* crediting the subdiscipline of Black psychology with being the initiator of this effort. The culture-specific approach to psychological research replaces the "deficit-deficiency models," which frame a universal reality based on White norms and values, without mention of time, place, context, or culture. White and Parham comment:

The development of an ethnic dimension in psychology suggested that other non-White Americans wanted to take the lead in defining themselves rather than continuing the process of being defined by the deficit-deficiency models of the majority culture. . . The evolution of the ethnic cultural perspective enlarged the scope of psychology. (p.10)

Given that ethnicity refers to groups defined by subcultural components such as religion, racial and national origin, as well as language (Harding, Kutner, Prohansky, and Chein, 1954), ethnic identity is self-conception associated with one or more of these components. The problem that arises is that traditional psychology emphasizes individuality -- the relationship between the mind and self. The vast amount of ethnic identity studies in psychology have been presented by social psychologists, such as George Herbert Mead (1909, 1910, 1913). Mead advanced a biosocial theory of the mind and self by proposing that inner consciousness is mediated by social behavior and interaction. Burkitt (1992) and Berger and Luckmann (1967) claim that the work of Mead (1913) resolved the separation between individual consciousness (self) and collective consciousness (society), suggesting that the personality is socially derived. The outstanding contribution Mead (1913) made was to connect the mind, self, society, language, discourse, and communicative activity within a unitary social psychological framework -- symbolic interactionism. One of the major criticisms of Mead's (1910, 1913) approach is raised by Farr (1990), who indicates that Mead claims to be a social psychologist but has directed his research toward sociology rather than social psychology; consequently the Chicago School has benefited more from his efforts. Still, contemporary social psychologists value Mead's (1909) initial theorizing in the field (Hewitt, 1988). Other social theories in the discipline besides symbolic interactionism include social learning theory (Bandura, 1971), social exchange theory (Blau, 1964; Homans, 1974), and phenomenology (Berger and Luckmann, 1967). Symbolic interactionism, however, is the most researched paradigm (Hewitt, 1988). Ethnic identity in psychology is discussed in some texts interchangeably as cultural identity. Yet ethnic identity is seen as a group phenomenon, socially and relationally driven (Goffman, 1959; Harre and Secord, 1972) and only to be understood from a social psychological perspective (J. Jones, 1991). While there is no specifically named ethnicity theory in psychology, there are ethnic (cultural) groups that have instituted their own psychological approaches, such as Black Psychology (White and Parham, 1990).

White and Parham discuss, in the vein of an ethnic orientation toward psychological research, coping strategies for a dual identity and social competency measures. The authors claim, "Long before the child can verbalize, he or she is aware of the fact that something is fundamentally wrong in the American society" (p. 45). While this point may be arguable, several ethnic identity models do propose that identity awareness begins in early to late adolescence. Thomas (1971), Cross (1971), Jackson (1976), and Banks (1981) offer four distinct models for examining ethnic identity growth among Blacks. The psychological paradigm discussed most in identity literature is Cross's nigrescence model. Cross's well-known theory (nigrescence meaning "to become Black"), virtually co-created by Thomas (1971), describes a metamorphosis from Negro to Black. A Negro in most literature since the 1960s has been defined as "the White man's artifact" (Fanon, 1967, p. 13) feeling forced to concede his "real self" in exchange for an "idealized self" (Horney, 1950, p. 42). Cross's (1971) definition of a Negro is no different; the Negro attempts to replicate behavioral patterns of Whites, especially White men (De Coy, 1987). In contrast, Black is defined as the optimal psychological stage, in which the Black individual comes to identify and appreciate who he or she really is. Persons at this stage do not consciously attempt to imitate another ethnic group's interpretation of reality.

There are four stages to the nigrescence model: pre-encounter, encounter, immersion-emersion, and internalization. The pre-encounter stage is the identity locale for those who embrace whiteness and devalue blackness. Thomas (1971) utilizes the term "negromachy" to characterize this stage. These persons refuse any link to a collective conscience or Black culture and have never been successfully influenced by Whites or themselves to accept their blackness. The encounter is the first instance or sequence of events in which the individual is confronted with an unfair situation because of his/her race. Due to the inconsistency of inequity with the American dream buttressed by "liberty and justice for all," the individual is initially shocked, then confronted with the realization that his/her present worldview is inappropriate. A new identity exploration gradually takes place; eventually the decision to maintain a Black identity is made. The immersion-emersion stage represents the transformation from the old to the new self. This transition is marked by an extremist viewpoint on Black-White relations. Whites are castigated for almost everything they do, while Blacks are praised. The world is now perceived from a Black-White perspective. Externally, artifacts of Black identity are worn or bought to decorate the home, car, office, etc. Internally, however, the individual has yet to become secure. Internalization is the final stage, in which the individual achieves a sense of self-comfort. Cross (1971) explains that the emotional and defensive disposition is exchanged for a politically acute awareness of other ideologies and a greater understanding of these views. Since 1971, Cross has published an updated version of the model and added internalization-committment as a final step in the process of nigrescence. This step explores issues of high and low race and culture salience, presuming that those who have matured to this stage are high in race and culture awareness.

Recently, Cross and Fhagen-Smith (1995) modified the nigrescence paradigm so that it accounts for ego identity development. One of the theoretic concerns of the authors relates to the range of identities and cultural ideologies of persons who have matured to the Internalization stage. The correlation between self-esteem, ego-identity development, and racial-cultural development greatly improves the nigrescence model. However, it may be possible that African Americans with a high self-esteem will have an enhanced sense of self-valuation due to a self-satisfaction and self-comfort with their present perception of their identities. The reformulation of the nigrescence theory significantly contributes to the advancement of identity studies by considering three dimensions of identity.

First, it accounts for multiple realities by considering the divergent ideologies of contemporary conservative leaders. Secondly, it includes cross-disciplinary research within the reconfiguration. Finally, it theoretically considers the outcome and process-oriented nature of identity throughout an entire lifespan.

White and Parham (1990) indicate that their concern for the nigrescence model is in its restricted focus on young adults and adolescents, with little to no regard for identity transitions later in life. Parham (1989) theorized that identity transformation is a lived experience beginning in adolescence and continuing throughout life. Nigrescence, then, is a cyclical occurrence that exists in early, middle, and late adulthood. "Recycling" of identity stages accounts for the individual moving back and forth between the stages. The heuristic contribution Parham (1989) provided was to conceptualize "African American cultural identity" as an independent phenomenon, not established as a reactive formation to White oppression. This discredits the notion established by Mintz and Price (1976) that African American culture evolved from slavery, suggesting that without slavery African American culture would not exist. Parham intuits that African American cultural identity is able to stand alone and function without a European American identity to claim and alter it.

Kovel (1984) speaks of a psychohistorical matrix confounded by an I-Other dialectic which has facilitated a link between culture and personality. The id, ego, superego, and culture are components of the matrix that forms self-concept. In the tradition of a universal psychological mandate for all personality formation, Kovel (1984) hypothesized that the ego is never satisfied. Progress is never achieved, but simply made -- the ego must continue making progress, extending its domain. Ani (1994), in response to Kovel, posits that the European self-image necessitates a parasitic I-Other orientation, which must have an inferior to which it relates as superior.

There have been three primary themes in Black psychological research -- inferiority, deficit/deficiency, and multicultural (White and Parham, 1990). The inferiority model asserts that hereditary factors render Blacks inferior to Whites. This inescapable predicament stagnates identity. The deficit/deficiency model suggests that race, class, gender, and other sociocultural factors distract societal members from adhering to normative standards of living, defined by the White middle class. These Black persons are "culturally deprived" due to assumed environmental conditions and a resilience to change. The deficiency lies in the inability of Blacks to reconcile their inherent lack of intelligence, sensible language, family structure, and cognitive style. The multicultural approach, the newest trend in psychological research, contends that all languages, behaviors, and worldviews are contextually related, and characterized by strengths and limitations. In the 1990s, ethnic identity research is primarily defined with respect to these three approaches within psychological literature.

Sociology

Sociologists have been preoccupied with issues of ethnic identity for decades (Berger and Luckmann, 1967; Hewitt, 1988; Ladner (ed.), 1998; Holzner and Robertson, 1979; Slugoski and Ginsburg, 1989; Tajfel, 1981; Tajfel, 1982). In 1979, Holzner and Robertson contended, however, "sociology in a general sense has not shown much concern with identity as a problem area. 'Identity' is not a core sociological concept in spite of its frequent occurrence in the everyday vocabulary of sociologists" (p. 2). These scholars further argued that ethnic identity has been discussed without any universal understanding of what the term means from one sociologist to the next. The identified void is clearly due to the lack of specificity and analytic attention given to the study of ethnic identity.

Hewitt (1988) addressed the early development of ethnic identity within role-playing behavior among children. Playing or enacting a role is described as being situationally defined. The work of Mead (1909, 1910, 1913) has been transferred to a generic, universalistic sociological theory, using the "I" and the *me* as theoretical referents. The "I" is the subject, and the "me" is the object. The difficulty is coordinating these two senses of self in order to share psychological space or identity locales. The individual's awareness of his or her own response signals the "me," within a given situation. The "I" exposes itself constantly, in everyday talk most often subconsciously. As each alternates, the conduct is coordinated accordingly. Social coordination is only possible via self-control.

Anselm Strauss (1978) contended that self-control is a manifested form of social order. This is described in his theory of negotiated order, which derives its roots from symbolic interactionism. Labor bargaining practices influenced the birth of Strauss's theory of regulated interaction, "negotiated order." Strauss postulated that deliberations proceed with an underlying awareness of norms, guidelines, and expectations of each party. Actions are mediated by a perceived need to coordinate social meanings and values. Within complex organizations, such as hospitals, government agencies, and universities, limitations are set, rules are interpreted, and exceptions are occasionally made. The first studies using negotiated order were within mental health facilities and were concerned with physician jurisdiction, doctor-patient relationships, and rule-abidance among employees. These agreements, according to Strauss, form an on-going process of negotiation. The contribution this model makes to social scientific and ethnic identity research is its potential to reinterpret identity as a relational negotiation process. Within sociology, social coordination is viewed as adequate role socialization, and knowledge of repercussions attached to deviant behavior.

Turner (1962) used two constructs to explain this coordination -- role-making and role-taking. "Role-making" is congruent to communication competence (Wiemann, 1977). It is the result of assessing a situation and assigning appropriate behavior to fit the situational demands. This process, according to Turner (1962), is consonant with one's own role and compliments the activity of others. "Role-taking," on the other hand, occurs when one occupies the role of another and assumes the other's perspective.

Berger and Luckmann (1967) instituted social constructionism as a method of "collective theorizing," through which a collective community creates and perpetuates conceptions of reality based on group experiences. Knowledge is socially negotiated and constituted, whereas social construction is ontologically defined. Emanating from Berger and Luckmann's (1967) approach is the ethogenic school initiated by British philosopher Rom Harre and American social psychologist Paul Secord (Harre and Secord, 1972). As noted earlier, ethogeny or ethogenic science describes the belief systems individuals use to derive meaning, assign patterns of behavior, as well as maintain their identities (Harre, 1979). Gergen (1994) argues that ethogeny is an amalgamation of language philosophy and structural anthropology, which contests the behavioral-deterministic model of psychology and endorses an examination of structured interaction patterns in everyday life.

Ethogenecists are contrasted by social identity theorists, who maintain a nominal group orientation. Tajfel (1981; 1982) and Turner (1968) described social categorization, a cognitive conception depicting the relationship between social patterns and personhood, coordinated in order to contrast self with others. Tajfel explains social categorization as "the ordering of social environment in terms of social groupings of persons in a manner which makes sense to the individual" (p. 61). Based on Turner's (1968) definition, social categorization is the framing of social identity within social groups. Gudykunst and Lim (1986) articulated social identity best: "The total of all social identifications individuals use to define themselves is their social identity, which is part of their self-concept" (p. 3). Self-invested societal memberships are equivalent to social identifications marked by a person's placement in social categories. Integration of social categorization with social identity encourages intergroup and interethnic distinctiveness.

The problem with these theories is their confinement to a socially driven capsule, with little regard for ethnicity or culture as a primary unit of identity analysis (Klapp, 1969; Robinson, 1978). Interethnic contact, perceived cultural similarity, intergroup attractiveness, and linguistic identity are research items produced by scholars from other disciplines (Berger and Bradac, 1982; Brewer and Campbell, 1976; Giles and Johnson, 1981; Gudykunst and Nishida, 1984).

Slugoski and Ginsburg (1989) endorsed Erikson's bipolar analysis of ethnic identity formation, consisting of Identity achievement and Identity diffusion. These two linguistic identity locales, on opposing ends of a continuum, represent an identity hierarchy. High-identity-status persons have achieved an enhanced internal locus of control and cognitive flexibility. Low-identity status, on the other hand, indicates a weak orientation toward self-control and a higher likelihood of a manipulated and diffused identity. The authors contend that identity achievement, however, is "in the final analysis an individual achievement" (p. 38). Regardless of the pressure to conform and establish a socially desirable identity (Goffman, 1959; Harre, 1979; Horwitz, 1975), Slugoski and Ginsburg defended the notion that high-identity (bourgeoisie) status is not only achievable but is also most readily attained following an identity crisis. The class-based perspective introduced by Erikson concludes that a competitive identity produces an individualist, and that the individualist is most likely to shift competently between different worlds, acquiring necessities for survival and self-comfort. "Self-comfort" means high-identity-status, a capitalistic interpretation of self-concept. The final tenet offered by Slugoski and Ginsburg suggests that one's sense of personal continuity is supported by a self-articulated identity derived from social networks, social conformity, and social institutions.

Several scholars assert that identity can best be studied within the constellation of race (ethnicity defined similarly), class, and identity (Bell, 1975; A. Davis, 1983; Freire, 1983; Glazer and Moynihan, 1975; Sowell, 1975; West, 1994). Paulo Freire (1983) explained the "survival-of-the-fittest" mentality differently than Slugoski and Ginsburg, in his *The Pedagogy of the Oppressed.* Freire posited that the oppressed individual becomes enthralled by a figure (i.e., Whites) deemed to be the apotheosis of freedom, self-contentment, and happiness. Consequently, the oppressor's identity is the object to be emulated and retained for self. "The oppressed suffer from a duality which has established itself in their innermost being" (p. 30). By identifying with the oppressor, the oppressed seek to escape the position of being threatened and acquire the capacity to threaten. Wilson (1990) diagnoses the ethnic identity complex by referring to the inferior/superior dialectic. The superior group (Whites) comprises those with privilege, seemingly just because they are White. The inferior group (Blacks) is underprivileged, and believed to be so because they are Black; therefore it is logical that the underprivileged will seek privilege by attempting to become White. Ture and Hamilton (1992) clearly argued that it is not that Blacks want to be White, but that Blacks want the power, privilege, and opportunity associated with whiteness, and some Blacks delude themselves into thinking it can be attained by incurring the pyscho-social manifestations of whiteness. Thus identity becomes situational, flexible, and opportunistic.

Communication

Identity research has been presented from differing perspectives, pivoting from one tenet: that identity is relational (Giles and Johnson, 1981; Hecht and Ribeau, 1984; Hecht et al., 1993; Hewstone and Jaspers, 1982; Hewstone and Brown, 1986; McCall and Simmons, 1978; Ting-Toomey, 1986). It is not stagnant but situated within the context of space, time, and circumstance (Wiemann, 1977). Stella Ting-Toomey posits that "the 'self' or 'identity' is refined and modified through the process of dyadic verbal and nonverbal negotiation" (p. 351). She further comments that identity is relational, reflexive, and multi-faceted. In 1986, Ting-Toomey created the identity validation model (IVM), which consists of three dimensions: identity-salience, perceived identity support, and communication. Role (group membership) identity and personal identity are the two poles on the continuum of low to high identity salience. "Role-identity salience" is described as a set of self-definitional cultural and social role identities. "Personal identity salience" refers to the significance one affixes to certain personal characteristics, such as weight, height, and hair texture. "Perceived identity support," according to Ting-Toomey (1986), is the validation of self-definition one receives from "relevant others" (p. 123). She further explains that two social or cultural group representatives are much more likely to initiate interaction after having perceived identity support. Communication is the final dimension, which is the actual "identity-negotiation process between the self and relevant others" (p. 123). This identity negotiation refers to the careful selection of one among several role identities to engage within a particular communication context.

Specifically, the author inquired about the type of individual that would initiate interpersonal ties. Four identity types were listed: balanced, personal, role, and marginal identifiers. "Balanced identifiers" are those who locate themselves high on the role and personal identity salience measures. In other words, they are communicatively competent, and have a high self-evaluation of their personal attributes. "Personal identifiers" are those who have a high self-evaluation but find themselves less competent at switching roles to accommodate others. "Role identifiers" are the opposite; they switch roles well but do not have a high self-esteem. "Marginal identifiers" are the final type, who define themselves as low on personal identity and role identity. Ting-Toomey concluded that balanced identifiers are most likely to initiate interpersonal ties among groups and that marginal identifiers are the least likely to initiate interaction. The identity validation model is the first interpretive framework found in the literature, which not only indicates that identity is relational but also explicitly notes that identity is a negotiated process. Uncertainty reduction theory (Berger and Calabrese, 1975) is the basis upon which Ting-Toomey's research on initial interaction is founded. However, negotiation was only considered a general phenomenon and not an actual construct in Berger and Calabrese's formula. Ting-Toomey proposed that future research examine the relational dilemmas and paradoxes that arise from members of two cultures "as they attempt to reach out and hold back at the same time, to seek for mutual validation, and yet at the same time to protect their own vulnerability" (p. 126).

Giles and Johnson (1981) posit that language identity has been scientifically undervalued and that no clear connection has been identified between language and ethnicity within communication research. The heuristic contribution made by the authors' theorizing is the link between ethnic and linguistic identity. These concepts are introduced as in-group and out-group experiences, which compel the group member to maintain ethnic group and language loyalty, alternatively labeled "ethnolinguistic vitality" (Giles et al., 1977). Language attitudes, roles, and interpretations are outlined in order to express linguistic distinctiveness. Giles et al. presented three categories influencing ethnolinguistic vitality: status, demographics, and institutional support. These authors mentioned institutions such as churches, schools, private industry, and government agencies. They further contend that the greater the institutional support, the linguistic population, and economic status, then the greater the vitality level among the members. Bourhis (1985) offered another set of terms to describe language loyalty: speech convergence and speech divergence. He argues that "speech convergence," or "codeswitching," is the result of utilizing the code of the dominant group, hence accommodating the more powerful group. "Speech divergence" is indicative of strong in-group loyalty, even at the cost of suffering repercussions for deviant behavior. Codeswitching was defined by Scotton (1988) as "the use of any two or more linguistic varieties in the same conversation, whether they are different languages, styles, or dialects" (p. 201). This broad definition encompasses lexical, syntax, and phoneme variation. When Scotton discussed style variation, she included references from a speaker's stylistic repertoire, which is indicative of that speaker's social experiences and ethnic group membership.

Ethnic identity among African Americans has probably been most comprehensively presented within the communication discipline by Michael Hecht, Mary Jane Collier, and Sidney Ribeau. While the authors provide ambiguous definitions of culture and ethnicity, the expansive amount of research presented in *African American Communication* is unsurpassed in identity research. There are more than fifteen studies by the authors alone, concluded by a communication theory of ethnic identity. A full explanation of their communication theory of ethnic identity is offered later in this chapter. One of the criticisms that immediately surfaces within this investigation is the authors' insistence on identifying African Americans as an ethnic group, and not a culture. Yet, interspersed throughout the book, culture is used as if it is a characteristic of African Americans, unlike ethnicity, which is paramount to their identity survival. Even recently, Martin, Hecht, and Larkey (1994) discuss the interethnic communication of African American and European American respondents.

CULTURE AND IDENTITY

Psychology

It was stated earlier that White and Parham (1990) emphatically reject self-hatred hypotheses; however, Karen Horney (1950) advanced beyond self-hatred models to "self-alienation." She explicated three self-conceived states of cultural identity negotiation -- the real, actual, and the idealized selves. Self-alienation is the prerequisite for each of these stages. The "real self" is the indigenous identity, optimal only because it fully represents the authentic totality of the individual. Additionally, it is the most distant from a neurotic or schizmic orientation. The "actual self" is the identity that one maintains at a given time and place. If applied to Turner's (1962) role-taking process, the actual self would be the most mobile identity, since the situation and identity change simultaneously. What an individual thinks he or she should be is characterized by the "idealized self." The "irrational imagination" induces the individual to abandon the real self , and identify with a false conception of self. White and Parham call this a "stagnated identity." Since the prerequisite is self-alienation, it logically follows that the real self moves away from self-alienation toward self-cohesion. The actual self is created by balancing who the self is at any given time. The idealized self, though, paralyzes itself in this state of self-alienation. Wilson (1990) considers self-alienation to be a formula which vacillates between the internal and external selves out of perceived necessity. This person is never defined by the real self; behavior is always determined by an externalized locus of control. The self is masked, or artificially presented in order to achieve a confirmation of his or her self-worth and self-definition. The alienated person is like Samaj's (1981) alien; confused, insecure, and dependent, constantly relying on others to direct self-activity and provide a sense of self.

Wilson argues that African American identity is riddled by the crucible of identity. Cultural symbols are deemed to be the nodal reference responsible for the shared establishment, perpetuation, and regulation of identity, behavior, and destiny. Any perceived threats yield a retaliatory response, yet interaction with European Americans contaminates the shared cultural bond, making it necessary to form in-groups and out-groups (Tajfel, 1981) and to alter symbol meanings as well as behavior. This marks the beginning of self-restriction and a reshaping of consciousness. Wilson explains that the group's viability and destiny lies in the hands of this alien entity, initially on a temporary basis, and that if not successfully resisted, the alien becomes the external locus of control indefinitely.

Any psychological interpretation of cultural identity must include a discussion of heroes, legends, myths, language systems, oral tradition, values, beliefs and ideals (Hare, 1991; Haskins and Butts, 1973; Welsing, 1991; White and Parham, 1990; Wilson, 1990). Black (African) psychology is a research area endorsed by a school of psychologists pioneered by Joseph White in 1970. A reprint of some of his groundbreakng work is presented in his 1991 book entitled *Toward a Black Psychology.* The psychological study of Blacks was deemed necessary in order to portray properly the mental health of African Americans. Some scholars argue that it is a reactionary statement to a White, hegemonic treatment of psychology (Guthrie, 1976). However, others contend that the necessity of Black psychology is much more penetrating than that (Akbar, 1991; Carruthers, 1972; Nobles, 1986; X et al., 1975). While not all African American psychologists support this paradigm, they do recognize the limitations of applying "Western" psychology to the experiences of African Americans (Baldwin et al., 1991).

Edwin Nichols (1976), an African American psychologist and organizational consultant in Washington D.C., proposed an outline known as the "psychological aspects of cultural difference" model. This framework for examining cultural distinctiveness includes the philosophical parameters of epistemology, axiology, and ontology. Moreover, it describes African American axiology as a "member-member" orientation as opposed to the European American "member-object" orientation. Member-member types are cultural representatives who value the relationship over materialistic acquisitions. The member-object types are those who relegate the relationship to a secondary position, making acquisition of the object primary. There have been several cultural theories depicting distinguished interpretations of reality. There has been some confusion over which model best measures cultural identity, but Burlew and Smith (1991) maintain that each approach is useful depending on the purpose of the research. The existing measures at the time were divided into four categories: developmental, africentric, group-based, and racial stereotyping approaches. "Developmental approaches" were exemplified by the process-oriented models of Thomas (1971), Cross (1971) and Milliones (1980). Milliones developed an instrument used to measure Black consciousness, foreshadowing Cross's nigrescence model by including the respondent's progression through four stages: preconscious, confrontation, internalization, and integration. The "africentric approaches" were typified by Baldwin's (1980) African self-consciousness scale, and the belief systems analysis scale of Montgomery, Fine, and James-Myers (1990). The latter scale was created to provide an optimal worldview which encouraged mental healthiness among African Americans. It is composed of three constructs: holistic, nonmaterialistic, and communalistic. The Black Group Identification Index is one of several "group" measures identified by Burlew and Smith (1991). This index was created by J.P. Davidson, a former doctoral student from the University of Maryland, who discovered a strong correlation between Black student identification and participation in extracurricular activities. Burlew and Smith also mention the Cultural Mistrust Inventory (Terrell and Terrell, 1981) as it relates to "racial stereotype" measures. This instrument was developed to assess the suspiciousness of Blacks toward Whites in workplace organizations. All of the aforementioned measures are significant methodological additions to identity research, yet they are only a few among many.

Harriet McCombs (1991) observes that self-concept has either been measured individually, as a personal achievement or collectively, as a racial group experience. Geert Hofstede (1980) first mentioned individualism and collectivism as cultural variables in *Culture-Consequences*. Individualism is considered a cultural phenomenon emphasizing personal goal achievement, while collectivism prioritizes the destiny of the collective. Nevertheless, in both situations, the interpretation of reality guides the research investigation. McCombs (1991) recommends a diunital approach like that of Dixon (1976) and calls it "individual/collective self concept." The author contends that the two are inseparable, since humans are both individuals and part of the collective at the same time. The ascribed membership associated with a given culture sacrifices choice. Consequently, African Americans cannot disengage themselves from their bio-physical characteristics, which readily locate them within a socially recognizable category (Goffman, 1959). Additionally, the individual cannot accurately represent the values and beliefs of every person in their cultural group.

Dixon's analysis is that worldview must recognize and appreciate others in order to be optimal. Either-or dichotomies force the self-concept into a confined prison for interpreting reality. Dixon suggests that it is not as parsimonious as delineating whether one is individualistic or collectivistic, acts Black or acts White. The writer identifies the hesitancy in scholarly acceptance of diunitality:

Euro-Americans, in turn, are less conscious of their dual existence in a union of opposites. They are more attuned to a sense of oneness, a sense of unitary existence. They perceive the American identity as their identity (p. 65).

Yet Dixon further notes that Blacks must strive to maintain their dual existence. Ogbonnaya (1994) explains the dual existence concept as an "intrapsychic community." Within this community, hierarchy is an anathema. The cultural self cohabitates with other selves in a community that affirms personhood. "The person grows by learning to harmonize these selves, not by making them uniform" (p. 82). Equality and subordinance are considered contrary to the concept of community. The person is a community of selves with an infinite possibility of multiple selves. Ogbonnaya criticizes the Freudian "self" as fragmented and inappropriate for a communitarian worldview. It assumes that pluralism handicaps the individual and proves their inability to function as an individual. The competitive ethos is said to be destroyed (p. 86).

Nobles (1991) asserts that Black psychologists should be concerned with replacing Western ideology with African cultural and philosophical premises. Liberation is key among Black psychology scholars. Critical psychological investigations of African American identity must be preoccupied with language, religion, customs, and behavior.

It has been suggested, however, that liberation of African Americans is only possible by first examining acculturation. Acculturation literature involves the extent to which ethnic and cultural groups participate in the traditions, values, beliefs, assumptions, and practices of the dominant White society. In 1994, two psychologists, Landrine and Klonoff developed the African American Acculturation Scale to examine eight aspects of African American culture: religion, family, socialization, food preparation and consumption, cultural artifacts, interracial attitudes, superstitions, and health beliefs and practices. The study concluded with a discussion of European American devaluation of African American cultural distinctiveness, and of the need to correct scientific misconceptions of African American culture and behavior.

Patti Lather (1992) discusses the interconnection between psychology and postmodernism. She explains that identity politics have been encapsulated in "webs of multiple representations of class, race, gender, language, and social relations" (p. 101). Postmodernists claim that each of these roles is understood differently by each individual within a given group. The most significant statement Lather (1992) makes in support of this investigation is that "self-identity is constituted and reconstituted relationally, its boundaries repeatedly remapped and renegotiated" (p. 101). She also asserts that identity is not static, but rather dynamic, process-oriented, and occasionally retrograde.

Sociology

Cultural notions of identity in sociology evolved from anthropological studies, where primitive societies, kinship systems, and culture were basic units of analysis (Barbu, 1971). Kroeber and Parsons (1958) were among the first social scientists to distinguish between culture and society. Culture was limited to patterns of behavior, symbols, values, and ideas. Society consisted of social systems, which were networks of interaction leading to the development of relationships.

Social science, as a discipline, originated from anthropology. Around the beginning of the twentieth century, sociology began as an academic discipline, growing out of social science. Social science included political economy, government, social studies, and history. Sociology became a hybrid research program coinciding with economics and the study of social problems. Du Bois was the first to lend intellectual attention to the problems of the Negro. In *The Philadelphia Negro,* Du Bois (1899) depicted issues of unemployment, poverty, and family disintegration, and charged Whites with an obligation to correct race prejudice and take responsibility for racial inequality. According to Rampersad (1976), Du Bois was convinced that an "aristocracy" of Black men, the "talented tenth," could meet and exceed the expectations of Whites who saw Blacks as intellectually impaired.

Du Bois's (1903) challenge to conduct objective race-relations research on the problems of the Negro was answered by Robert Park. That liberal American sociologist was the leading scholar in the development of the sociology discipline during the 1920s and 1930s (Lyman, 1972). He concerned himself with issues of race prejudice and discrimination. Under his tutelage came Black sociologists Charles S. Johnson, E. Franklin Frazier, Bertram Doyle, and St. Clair Drake (Bracey, Meier, and Rudwick, 1973). These scholars were inspired to conduct race relations research as well. Park (1950), however, never intended for his research to espouse a theme of racial and economic equality. He was primarily interested in the socioeconomic hierarchy that he believed resulted from racial contact. According to Bracey et al. (1973), Park (1950) theorized that conflict and competition were inevitable whenever races interacted. Moreover, the conflict could only be resolved by one race occupying a superior position over another; this, he called the "etiquette of race relations" (p. 13). The dominant group would exercise control over the powerless minority, who would be forced to accommodate and eventually assimilate.

Ralph Ellison (1973) maintained that this prediction was carried on later by the internationally renowned Swedish economist, banker, and government advisor Gunnar Myrdal (1944), who concluded after a five-year study: "It is to the advantage of American Negroes as individuals and as a group to be assimilated into American culture, to acquire the traits held in esteem by the dominant white Americans" (p. 4). Ellison (1973) explicitly rejected Myrdal's view of "Negro culture and personality" (p. 94) as socially pathological, a reactionary self-concept grown out of oppression and contingent upon White acceptance.

This refusal of an independent, self-sustaining African American culture inspired a greater emphasis on African American culture within sociological studies. W.E.B. Du Bois, the first African American sociologist, along with Drake, Frazier, Doyle and Johnson was among the early sociologists who set a foundation from which Black sociology was to emerge (Omi and Winant, 1986). Joyce Ladner (1973), editor of *The Death of White Sociology,* anthologized the ideas of Black sociology proponents into a single volume. Robert Staples was one of those advocates. He characterized Black sociology as a "sociology of Black liberation," charging White sociology with promoting and institutionalizing racist ideologies and practices. Commenting on classical sociologists such as August Comte, Franklin Giddings, Herbert Spencer, and William Sumner, Staples (1973) argued that racial segregation and injustice was justified. He contends that White sociology has failed in its attempt to explain the Black experience, since Whites have never shared the socioeconomic experiences of Blacks. The basis for a school of Black sociology evolves from the need to socially and historically critique Black institutions and behavior, as well as the extent to which they benefit the collective community. The Black masses, according to Staples, are best served by a community of scholars who are both activists and academicians. Names that have been used to describe this new vanguard are "organic intellectuals" and "scholar-activists." These cultural workers have arranged themselves in various academic circles and organizations, and have aligned themselves with causes consistent with liberationist perspectives.

Communication

Pajaczkowska and Young (1992) assume that White identity has an absent center, due to a reliance on socioeconomic comparison. The authors posit that a colonialistic, power-based identity never has to define its parameters and therefore exists without boundaries. It is only when scientific inquiry evokes historical referents that White identity becomes problematic. Its blankness is concealed by the substance of the "other."

Asante (1980) proposed a culture-specific approach to self-analysis. African descendants are encouraged to appreciate other cultures, while placing African ideas, communication, values, beliefs, customs, and patterns of behavior at the center of one's interpretation of reality. This readjustment from margin to center is critical to self-understanding and self-construal (Kim and Sharkey, 1995). Watzlawick, Beavin, and Jackson (1967) posited that "one cannot not communicate" (p. 51) and that therefore communication is inevitable. Hecht and Ribeau (1984) claimed that identity is communicated via interaction; consequently, identity is a process of message exchange. Inasmuch as each individual has multiple and shifting identities (Collier and Thomas, 1988) present in everyday talk, (Goffman, 1959) cultural identity is only one of several. Kluckhohn and Strodtbeck (1961) noted that culture is a "design for living," a "value-orientation," which introduces a worldview. Hofstede (1980) mentions individualism-collectivism as an index for measuring variegated cultural dimensions.

Kim and Sharkey examine interaction constraints within pluralistic workplace organizations using an individualistic-collectivistic equivalent, identified by the authors as independent and interdependent self-construals. The terms are reconceptualized because of their generality. The research investigated three concerns: for clarity; for avoiding hurting the hearer's feeling; and for avoiding negative evaluation by the hearer. The two dimensions of independent and interdependent construals of self prove to be useful, since they account for an individual self-concept and a personality of the collective. The results of the study indicate that cultural self-construals are directly related to a perceived importance of clarity, efforts to avoid hurting others' feelings, and avoidance of negative evaluation.

Collier and Thomas (1988) offered a rules-theory approach to studying culture, personality, and communication. They recommended that cultural identity be studied as one among many negotiated identities, not independently managed. The theory is presented as a set of six assumptions, five axioms and one theorem. Intercultural competence facilitates the negotiation and validation of cultural identity. Thus, the negotiation is mediated by discursive management. Cultural identity varies according to the scope, salience, and intensity of attributed and avowed identities. The authors suggested a correlation between these three dimensions and the degree of intercultural communication competence. The highest competence is achieved when the interactant's attributed identity for their partner is consistent with their partner's avowed identity. Rubin and Martin (1994) provided the most detailed instrument now available for measuring intercultural communication competence; it includes the following constructs: empathy, self-disclosure, social relaxation, assertiveness, interaction management, altercentrism, expressiveness, supportiveness, immediacy, and environmental control. Rubin and Martin define intercultural communication competence as "an impression or judgment formed about a person's ability to manage interpersonal relationships in communication settings" (p. 33). Initially, communication competence was used by intercultural researchers to lessen the intergroup contact effect of culture shock (Oberg, 1960), and ensure a "smooth and successful interaction" (Cupach and Spitzberg, 1983, p. 565) among culturally distinct interlocutors (Hammer, 1989).

Communication patterns are adapted in order to establish appropriate and effective interpersonal ties among interactants (Ting-Toomey, 1986). Adaptation, accommodation, and acculturation literatures have contributed to the evolution of cultural identity studies within the field of communication (Dyal and Dyal, 1981; Gallois et al., 1988; Kim, 1986; Ting-Toomey, 1986; Ting-Toomey, 1989). The studies of immigrants and sojourners' adaptation and communication conflict (Kim, 1989); acculturative stress (Dyal and Dyal, 1981) interpersonal bonding across intergroup boundaries (Ting-Toomey, 1986;1989); as well as group affiliation and accommodation (Gallois et al., 1988) have all heuristically advanced identity research. Also, these publications have necessitated an investigation to examine systematically the negotiation of cultural identity from an interpretive perspective.

Third Culture Building is one of the few process models which considers culture and identity within the same framework. The theory postulated by Starosta and Olorunnisola (Chen and Starosta, 1998) offers the flexibility to trace the development of multiple identities or a single identity. Hecht et al.'s (1993) communication theory of ethnic identity, while not a process model, thoroughly explains ethnic-cultural identity but seems to obfuscate the terms "culture" and "ethnicity." Hecht has created a valuable tradition of African American identity research, which has consistently observed ethnic identity as inherently relational, managed, and negotiated (Hecht, 1993; Hecht and Ribeau, 1984; Hecht, Collier, and Ribeau, 1993; Hecht, Ribeau, and Alberts, 1989; Martin, Hecht, and Larkey, 1994).

CHAPTER SNAPSHOT

This chapter is organized to facilitate the reader's ability to trace the evolution and conceptual development of identity studies across three disciplines as they relate to race, ethnicity, and culture. The identity literatures of the sociology, psychology, and communication disciplines were examined under each of these headings.

The three literature reviews surveyed the research, theories, and models which purport to examine identity as it relates to race, ethnicity, and culture, respectively. As you have read, there are certainly many paradigms which are designed to measure or explain racial, ethnic and cultural self-definition. This list is not meant to be exhaustive. In an intellectual age where cultural research is so prevalent, it would be greatly presumptuous of any researcher to lay claim to an exhaustive list of perspectives. But the ones herein offer a "smorgasbord" for those interested in exploring the spate of identity studies.

Chapter 5

Two Theories of Communicated Identity

Two existing paradigms form the core of this investigation: the third culture building model and the communication theory of ethnic identity. Chapter 1 identified the elements to be applied here from each paradigm, the following explanation gives a full description of each perspective.

THIRD CULTURE BUILDING

This model was developed in the early 1990s by a communication professor, William Starosta, and his graduate student at the time, Anthony Olorunnisola, at Howard University; prior to the study presented in this book it had not been empirically tested or verified. The achieved objective of these scholars was to provide an heuristic advancement in the study of intercultural communication. The meta-model is quite reminiscent of language metamorphosis, in that all languages are said to be "pidgins" in their infancy stages of development and then to mature into "creoles"; subsequently they become a fully functional language.

The process here appears to be a communicologist's reinterpretation of that metaphorphosis, in addition to a combination of equity theory and a phenomenological approach to the study of intercultural communication. Nonetheless, this nascent metatheory, Third Culture Building (TCB), should be lauded for its recognition that intercultural communication encompasses several gradations ranging from micro (individual) to macro (societal) levels of communication analysis. According to Hecht et al. (1993), identity exists on multiple levels as well (see Figure 5.1) and deserves an identical examination, one that is contextually based, in order to include the back and forth movement of identity-shifting. One of the contributions the TCB model makes is to specify the levels of communication -- intracultural, interpersonal, rhetorical, and mass media. These sub-disciplinary perspectives are included in a comprehensive framework for examining "A process by which two or more entities come to take account of each other, to extract and to process messages from the other, and ultimately to respond to the symbolic realities of another entity who has been differentially socialized (Chen and Starosta , 1998)."

Figure 5.1
Meta-Model for the Development of a Third Culture

T1: Unilateral Awareness.	A notices B.
T2: Unilateral Presentation.	A makes self known to B.
T3: Inquiry.	A seeks info. about B.
T4: Reciprocation.	A engages B in processes already described.
T5: Mutual Adjustment.	A and B start to question their values, mores and attitudes as they relate to the other.
T6: Convergence.	A and B replace some attitudes, mores and values and modify others to more nearly resemble the other.
T7: Reconfiguration.	A and B integrate new and revised attitudes, mores and values into existing constellations.
T8: Readjustment/Reinforcement.	A and B renegotiate their relationship in light of changing circumstances and contexts.
T9: Mutual Assimilation.	Some of these renegotiated aspects of the relationship become permanent and self-perpetuating.
T10: Separation from Primary Culture.	A and B adopt the revised identity as their primary identity and transmit their new identity to a subsequent generation.

To review, the authors suggest that this interaction process can be either voluntary or coerced, with ephemeral or enduring effects, across or within national boundaries. One unambiguous aspect of this negotiation, however is that it is considered a conscious exchange in which the interactants are privy to their participation. An interesting characteristic the authors include is that the process may be intentional for both parties or only one. In other words, Watzlawick, Beavin, and Jackson's (1967) theme, "One cannot not communicate," applies here. Communication is inevitable, constantly occurring, providing a context for negotiation even without the consent of all parties involved. The model includes ten stages, presented in chronological order. The first stage occurs in all intercultural episodes, but the latter stages may not be reached due to a discontinuity in the communication process. The stages are unilateral awareness, unilateral presentation, inquiry, reciprocation, mutual adjustment, convergence, reconfiguration, readjustment/reinforcement, mutual assimilation, and separation from primary culture.

The first stage is "unilateral awareness," in which two individuals recognize the other's cultural group and begin to consider some basis for interaction. The motivation may be simply inquisitive reasons or "the wish to influence another person in a way that better serves the mutual interest of the two parties." This stage is described as potentially a preconscious process, one that precedes the declaration of a specific or general purpose, such as courtship or information-gathering. In brief, it is the "sizing-up" component of TCB in which the communicants decide if the other is worthy of consideration. The second stage is "unilateral presentation." The first two stages are given the collective appellation "Intracultural Intrapersonal Communication." Within this second stage, at least one of the individuals initiates interaction. A few examples given are a phone call, a letter, or any dialogue that introduces one person to the other. This is considered a mutual exchange, which may promote or discourage future discourse but does not involve any cultural adjustment except a search for a linguistic medium that facilitates understanding between both parties. There is a conscious decision by at least one of the parties to attempt to confirm or disqualify rather elaborate internal skepticism about the other. (This reverberation of Delia and Clark's [1977] "cognitive complexity" is alternatively labeled "higher awareness.") Such reservations might manifest themselves in the form of stereotypes regarding the extent to which the other is helpful or condescending, for example. First impressions and intuitive feelings are invaluable at this point and preface the remainder of the negotiation process. The third, fourth, and fifth stages are under the rubric of "interpersonal/intercultural communication."

The third stage is "inquiry," which begins when the presenter seeks information about the message recipient as a cultural representative, in order to decipher the other's degree of commitment to a group-based or individually based center of meaning. This is a continual activity that contributes to the development and well-being of a healthy relationship. The next stage, "reciprocation," allows for the message recipient to engage in the same process of inquiry, thus moving the interaction to an interpersonal level. Up to this point, if communication has not been terminated, both parties are considered highly tolerant of ambiguities and willing to engage one another in discourse regardless of potential imparity or "asymmetry." Furthermore, each stage is cumulative, therefore in order for one to arrive at stage four, he or she must have already experienced all prior stages. The fifth stage is "mutual adjustment," which presupposes that each party is willing to interact in a fair and equitable manner, or else the possibility for further contact will be eliminated. Inequitable acts include colonization, exploitation, or degradation, according to the authors. Within this phase each interactant begins questioning his or her own values, mores, and attitudes. Thereafter each party comfortably continues, even if one has a different set of motives than the other. As long as both are satisfied with interaction up to this point, progress will persist.

Two examples furnished by the authors are friendship and bilateral negotiations, with certain exceptions, such as having a preconceived understanding of an identical agenda. The initiator's present and past behaviors are under scrutiny by the recipient. The acceptance of the initiator's initial invitation to engage may seem to be enough for adjustment, but the authors indicate otherwise. The need to assess the initiator's worthiness must be met in order to further develop a relationship. The recipient is also placed under similar scrutiny. This is the genesis of the actual third-culture creation. As the interactants question their own cultures, they seek to eliminate those cultural constructions, preferences, and practices not feasible for inclusion in a third culture. The authors advise that honesty is essential, since the third culture is predicated on these initial considerations. The potency of each ingredient is managed in regard to the final product and long-term consequences associated with it. Each individual is not only preoccupied with his or her own culture but also the other's culture and its contributions.

The sixth stage is "convergence"; this phase and the next are under the heading of "rhetorical/intercultural communication." At the time of convergence, both parties are more cognizant of differences and choose to value these distinctions as respectable alternative realities. This viewing of the other's culture in a positive light is the crux of convergence. The establishment of a third culture requires that this stage reflect adjustments and abandonment of previously identified cultural discrepancies that may hinder progress. Convergence, described as emotion-laden, can be understood as the interactants' attempt to "balance" cultural indices as though they were "ledger items." Dissimilarity is reduced significantly, and too much cultural variance is discouraged. The assumption is that there is a direct relationship between the amount of information exchange and the likelihood of achieving a third culture perspective. "Integration" is the true negotiation phase, in which all extracted cultural indices are synthesized and theoretically organized into a new third perspective. Some revisions of previously held attitudes, mores, and values are part and parcel to this amalgamation. The initiator and recipient eliminate any flaws or apparent oversights admitted in prior concessions. Further modifications may occur in later stages, due to the theoretical nature of this component of the TCB model.

"Readjustment/Reinforcement" is the beginning of what is known as "metacultural communication." The third culture, now constructed, is rearranged in order to achieve a best fit. The two parties begin to enact the roles, expectations, and agreements which were discussed and adopted. The contextual appropriateness and overall workability of the arrangement are critically examined. The perpetuation and self-regulation of the third culture perspective is viewed as a system with interdependent parts that must maintain balance in order to thrive successfully. Reinforcement is a vital facet of TCB, since it excludes the possibility of the abandoned culture's beliefs, values, and mores interfering with the newly decided cultural indices. "Mutual assimilation" is the ninth stage of TCB, and at this point certain elements are established, consistent, and perpetuating. The decline of divergent norms and rules is readily apparent. The final stage is "primary culture abandonment" or "Separation from Primary Culture." No matter how it is named, the disconnection with one's original culture is clear. The new primary culture is the mutually agreed-upon version of reality understood and lived by both parties. The model completes the circle of communication by returning to an internal examination of self -- "intrapersonal communication" (see Figure 5.2). The authors offer tables to accompany the theory to elaborate on exceptions, effects, progressions, and roles of the interactants.

Figure 5.2
Phases of Third Culture Development Cycle

> *Intrapersonal / Intracultural Communication*
>   Unilateral Awareness
>   Unilateral Presentation
> *Interpersonal / Intercultural Communication*
>   Inquiry
>   Reciprocation
>   Mutual Adjustment
> *Rhetorical / Intercultural Communication*
>   Convergence
>   Reconfiguration
> *Metacultural Communication*
>   Readjustment
>   Mutual Assimilation
> *Intracultural Communication*
>   Primary Culture Abandonment

Third Culture Building is an intricate process that combines negotiation and intercultural communication into a comprehensive framework for understanding negotiation as a (communication) process. The TCB model is particularly useful to this investigation, since it proposes that two individuals can make contact with one another and perhaps arrive at a stage in their relationship where they are willing to question their values, mores, and beliefs (i.e., components of their cultural identities); furthermore, these two may attempt to alter their values in order to resemble more closely the other. Immediately, the question arises: Is this just a marginalized group phenomenon, or does this also happen to European Americans? If European Americans do experience this negotiation of cultural identity, this investigation explores to what extent context plays a part in determining the outcome of the negotiation process.

COMMUNICATION THEORY OF ETHNIC IDENTITY

Michael Hecht, Mary Jane Collier, and Sidney Ribeau (1993) present a communication-oriented perspective to the study of ethnic identity as it relates to African Americans. Collier and Thomas's (1988) "Cultural Identity Theory" proposed the relationship between intercultural competence and cultural identity. Hecht, Collier and Ribeau (1993) provide an heuristic contribution to the discipline of intercultural communication by applying this linkage to African Americans. Moreover, the expansion of Collier and Thomas's (1988) theory included an interpretation of African American identity based on core symbols, prescriptions, code, conversation, and community. Community encompasses ritual, myth, and social drama. Frames and assumptions of identity accompany the recently devised paradigm. According to the authors, African Americans identify with an ethnic culture, a social organization with a common sense of ancestry, tradition, aesthetics, and values that coalesce around racial characteristics. For ease of terminology we will call the sense of belonging to an ethnic culture "ethnic identity" (Hecht, Collier and Ribeau, 1993). The research presented in their book concurs with the TCB model, in that it is explicitly stated that identity creates and is co-created by people who come in contact with one another and align themselves within a mutual context or environment, so that symbols, meanings, norms, and realities are shared. The explanation of ethnic culture suggests that ethnic identity is directly related to the actor's social construction of meaning. This notion coincides with the definition of culture used within this investigation, and borrowed from Wade Nobles: "Culture is a process which gives people a general design, and patterns for interpreting their reality" (p. 17). The problem is that Hecht, Collier, and Ribeau (1993) are discussing something a little different than cultural identity. (N.B. an explanation of race, ethnicity, and culture can be found at the beginning of Chapter 2.) They are investigating ethnic identity, which can include religious groups or any co-cultural arrangement where a group alliance and history is present.

To be a member of a culture is to be an active participant in an on-going social construction process, where race is only one binding factor. The meaning-centered *process* is primary in differentiating race, ethnicity, and culture. Thus, to say that one is negotiating cultural identity is to say that one's process of interpreting reality is being considered for reconstruction and redefinition. The communication theory of ethnic identity, while it concerns itself with group member enrollment and allegiances, also considers the basic premise that identity is inherently an interactive process. This premise is consistent with the ideas presented in this investigation. A communication interpretation of identity regards it as a set of symbolic messages that are exchanged, altered, and negotiated depending on the communication role, context, and people involved. Identity is described as a code for being, providing a capsule for understanding how one defines oneself, and one's place in a community of interactants. One's ability to define self (i.e., identity) predetermines conduct; consequently who one thinks he or she is relates to what one thinks one should be doing. Self-definition is not to be confused with Maslow's self-actualization. It is quite possible for one to interpret one's own worldview without having been fully self-actualized. A few sensitizing concepts are listed, which are indicators of identity, and they are as follows: core symbols, prescriptions, code, conversation, and community. These are the bases for the authors communication theory of ethnic identity.

"Core symbols" are the conduit through which cultural members express themselves, their beliefs, values, and personhood. The core symbols illustrate one's interpretations, definitions, and boundaries for living, and are the actual building blocks in the social construction of meaning. Epistemologically, this facet explains what one needs to know to identify with and claim membership in an ethnic culture (i.e., a cultural group). Hecht et al. (1993) consider ethnic culture to be a system of rules governing proper behavior and a shared understanding of "the way things are" (Geertz, 1973). Interpretations and patterns of conduct are vital ingredients in any definition of culture; thus ethnic culture and culture, within this investigation, are synonymous terms. The core symbols are central features of an ethnic culture and are identified over a period of time after "recurrent patterns" (Hecht, et. al., p. 23) of message exchange or interaction have emerged. For example, power has historically been identified as a core symbol for analyzing race and cultural identity issues (Carmichael and Hamilton, 1967/1992; DeCoy, 1987; Fanon, 1963). "Prescriptions" are previously decided and agreed upon guidelines for appropriate and competent behavior. This includes moral regulations and an aesthetic disposition. Philosophically, prescriptions would be categorized as an axiological construct. When considering one's sense of whom he or she is, an individual cannot ignore the fundamental values that underpin behavior and moral conscience. Competence is an additional dimension to prescription. It is necessary that one acquires the knowledge, skills, and motivation for effective execution of prescribed behavior. Competence is a significant expectation one must fulfill in order to be considered normal within a given culture. Communication becomes problematic when interaction is not only intracultural but also intercultural. The systems of rules, prescriptions, symbols, and behavioral norms will most likely differ, thus causing some dissonance. Identity is defined differently; therefore interpretations, values, beliefs, and meanings are construed differently. Competence becomes tremendously more complex, and the variables are much more intricate. Competence is definitely related to the perceived necessity of code switching behavior among African Americans. "Code" is the third "sensitizing construct." It is the first of the three constructs borrowed from Gerry Philipsen's (1987) work on cross-cultural communication. "Codes" are a set of symbols and meanings manifested in linguistic devices for coordinating language choice, guiding language patterns, and maintaining social order. Codes are equivalent to codes of conduct, which determine normal and acceptable behavior within a certain sociocultural milieux (i.e., code switching). "Conversation" is an interaction, which may or may not be episodic. The conversation can continue as long as two or more individuals are present. The patterns of interaction, the rules governing the interaction, and the social pressures to conform to ritual exchanges in certain contexts describe the elements of conversation. "Community" is the final construct of the Communication Theory of Ethnic Identity. Community involves a shared, collective, and widely recognized set of understandings held by a group with an unlimited number of members. It is assumed that the group is connected by a conjoint identity and setting, and driven by a common use of symbols, meanings, norms, and prescribed codes (see Figure 5.3).

Ritual, myth, and drama are three additional forms of cultural communication instituted by Philipsen (1987). Each of these contributes to a strong in-group cohesion. Ritual refers to routine, structure, and patterns of behavior. Over time, rituals become almost second-nature to indigenous members of a given culture. They solidify nuances and tendencies particular to he cultural community. Playing the dozens is one such ritual; signification is another. Myths are symbol-filled social constructions that support a past, present and/or future reality for the collective. As a form of social reality, members learn values, establish heroes, and maintain codes of conduct through the telling of narratives. The myths are carried on from one generation to the

Figure 5.3
Communication Theory of Ethnic Identity (Truncated)

Core symbols:	expressions of cultural beliefs and understandings.
Prescriptions:	rules guiding behavior and appropriate conduct.
Code:	a set of symbols and meanings based on a worldview.
Conversation:	express patterns of social interaction or discourse.
Community:	that which defines racial, ethnic, and cultural membership.

Note: This figure represents Hecht, Collier & Ribeau's Relevant Sensitizing Constructs.

next; in some African cultures, the griot is the appointed storyteller for the community. In African American culture, the myths of Shine and Stagolee are common examples. Drama is the enacted script or prescript within a given community. Standards and roles are key elements in institutional dramas, and facilitate the establishment of leadership. There may be certain exceptions to the rules, but there emerges a clear distinction between acceptable and unacceptable conduct. The drama is the evolutionary stage that transcends theory, and illustrates the practical dimension of reality. Ritual, myth, and drama highlight the everyday interaction among cultural members. The conjoined union of these group members creates a strong interdependent network of individuals, who move toward greater and greater exclusivity. Their culture defines its own boundaries, consequently excluding others who hold divergent mores, customs, attitudes, and beliefs. Tajfel (1981) would describe this as an in-group/out-group phenomenon.

There are several frames of reference which provide the "location" of identity. Hecht, Collier & Ribeau suggest that identity exists within individuals, relationships, and groups. This theory endorses an interpretive analysis of cultural identity which hypothesizes that individuals create their identity, and relationally express, define, and negotiate their identities with others. These frames are not isolated, but occur simultaneously. Thus, they are called "interpenetrating frames." There are eight overall assumptions and nine more specific assumptions related to frames. Only the eight overall assumptions are critical for this study, as outlined by Hecht et al. (1993, p. 166). These are as follows:

1. Identities have individual, enacted, relational and communal properties.
2. Identities are both enduring and changing.
3. Identities are affective, cognitive, behavioral, and spiritual.
4. Identities have both content and relationship levels of communication.
5. Identities involve both subjective and prescribed meanings.
6. Identities are codes expressed in conversation, and define memberships in communities.
7. Identities have semantic properties that are expressed in core symbols, meanings, and labels.
8. Identities describe modes of appropriate and effective communication.

Core symbols, prescriptions, code, conversation, and community are the five sensitizing constructs presented by Hecht et al. (1993) in their introduction of a Communication Theory of Ethnic Identity. Core symbols such as power influence the maintenance and development of cultural identity. Prescribed rules of conduct determine what linguistic choices are made in a given context. Code involves the establishment of standards that are to be maintained by cultural members and must be enacted within an appropriate context. Code switching describes adherence to norms as related to code and context variation. Conversation includes the language choices but focuses on patterns of interaction that persist over time. These aforementioned constructs must be shared by a community of interactants in order for there to be a common understanding of appropriateness from one person to the next.

For this investigation, the core symbols, prescriptions, codes, conversations, and communities will be identified by the focus group interviewees. The recurring patterns of response, after having been communicated, will be used to derive categories. Themes will be allowed to emerge as a result of the focus group interviews, which is indicative of interpretive research. The underlying frames and assumptions are the guiding tenets for the investigation.

CHAPTER SNAPSHOT

This chapter presents a description of two paradigms used in this research, TCB and CTEI. A truncated form of these theories is offered in Chapter 1 and presented in figures 1, 2, and 3 of this chapter.

This chapter testifies to a dearth of research that systematically examines identity negotiation among African Americans. Many authors discuss issues surrounding identity as a non-cultural concept; very few, however, discuss cultural identity as not only a communication-driven phenomenon but also as a negotiation process. Stella Ting-Toomey (1989), Hecht and his associates (1993), and Starosta and Olorunnisola (Chen and Starosta, 1998) most clearly articulate the communication and bargaining aspects of cultural identity. Yet, empirical evidence of these authors' theorizing has been limited, and communication, culture, identity and negotiation have not been presented as salient constructs within the same theoretical space.

Chapter 6

Research Design and Methodology

Scientists firmly believe that as long as they are not conscious of any bias or political agenda, they are neutral and objective, when in fact they are only unconscious. (Namenwirth, 1986, p.29)

Namenwirth (1986), in *Feminist Approaches to Science*, convincingly argues, in a Socratic vein of thinking, that the greatest knowledge is gained by recognizing that one knows nothing. This statement refutes the notion that scientific inquiry enhances predictability by translating human action into precise and measurable units. Namenwirth further asserts that pure objectivity is impossible -- bias always exists (p. 30). Research bias and data collection are two of the prominent issues discussed in this chapter. Other significant components covered include recruitment and descriptions of interviewees, research questions, interview guide protocols, and explanations of focus group interviews.

Research bias has been an academic concern for decades, primarily because truth in science is intersubjective (Reinharz, 1983; Smith, 1988). When a community of scholars, using empirically proven and self-correcting measures, agrees that something exists, it is considered to be objective scientific knowledge (Kerlinger, 1986). Interpretive research recognizes the bias inherent within scientific inquiry and seeks to minimize researcher bias by relying upon the subject to interpret his/her own reality and using direct quotations to express how meaning is construed (Lincoln and Guba, 1985).

Predictions in a qualitative paradigm are tested via several data collection techniques. The method used in the present study is focus-group interviewing, which is augmented by data-collection via a fourteen-item survey. This secondary technique is implemented to confirm the results of the primary method employed -- the focus group interviews. After each of the two nonscheduled interviews, the researcher will determine a posteriori categories, with themes already identified by the participant. The primary difference between the scheduled and nonscheduled interview is with the interview protocol. The scheduled interview represents the most structured set of questions, most often used when several interviewers are needed to maintain consistency of response. For example, McCracken (1988) indicates that if a respondent is uncertain about a question and needs clarification, the interviewer is trained simply to repeat the question. In a nonscheduled interview, an interview guide is often used, which facilitates flexibility in the order and manner in which a question is asked. This is preferred by researchers with three or fewer interview facilitators, and can potentially yield greater detail (R. Jones, 1985).

Many researchers are confounded by the differences between the functionalist and interpretivist paradigms. Both perspectives are useful in context, and when combined they offer a powerful triangulated approach for studying the changing nature of human interaction.

Thomas Kuhn (1970) explained that knowledge changes consistently with the conditions of those who construct it. Consequently, ideology and meaning are intertwined. As social constructionist Patti Lather (1992) posits, no meaning exists outside of ideology. Lindlof (1995) explains that many communication scholars refuse to recognize interpretive research as normal science, because it does not admit objectivity as a primary research goal. Lindlof (1995) outlines several scientific qualitative methods and offers explicit support of "interpretive inquiry as a coherent way of studying communication" (p. 30).

The principal strength of functionalist inquiry is predictability, which is instrumental for theory construction. The major weakness of the functionalist approach, however, is its treatment of human interaction. Infante et al. (1990) assert that this paradigm suggests that social interaction can be understood in general, when in fact communication episodes are individualized events influenced by context. According to McCracken (1988), the goal of quantitative research is "to isolate and define categories as precisely as possible *before* the study is undertaken, and then to determine again with great precision, the relationship between them" (p. 16).

In discussing the interpretive paradigm, Littlejohn (1992) notes, "The goal of interpretive theories is not to posit laws that govern events, but to uncover the ways in which people actually understand their own experience or the meanings within texts and the objects of interpretation" (p. 15). Shimanoff (1980) contended that the true nature of reality can be found in subjective experience. The rules and norms guiding behavior, Shimanoff intuited, are often interpreted differently among individuals.

Geertz (1973) endorsed Shimanoff's perspective and also challenged social scientific researchers to use a "thick description" (Ryle, 1949) or idiographic orientation when studying human communication behavior. Geertz (1973) describes thick descriptiveness as a subjective version of reality that represents the often unnoticed daily intricacies of behavior. Thick ethnographic data is the rich description of a chain of events experienced and recounted by the individual.

The major strength of this paradigm is its concern for human choice, and free will, and its recognition of differing interpretations of environmental stimuli within context. This perspective is also valuable since it critically assesses meaning from the perspective of the interactant and not from an etic perspective. The most outstanding weakness is the inability to extrapolate findings to a larger population, as a result of which predictability is also sacrificed. The goal of qualitative research is to "isolate and define categories *during* the process of research" (McCracken, 1988, p. 16).

RECRUITMENT OF RESPONDENTS

The respondents for the focus groups were a convenience sample. I personally invited participation by distributing and posting flyers; the posting was made accessible to the entire student population at both Pacifica and Atlantica universities. In addition, participants were expected to meet several criteria (See Figure 6.1).

Figure 6.1
Eligibility for Focus Group Participation

1. One year at selected post-secondary institution
2. Atlantica Citizenship
3. Self-reported cultural affiliation was either European or African American
4. Voluntary Participation
5. Availability for a full one-hour focus group

The flyers were posted on bulletin boards, in convenient locations such as cafeterias, classrooms, and residence halls and were handed out during lunch hour. In most cases, initial contact was not made via a posted flyer, but rather in person. If a respondent was recruited by a posted flyer I spoke to him or her initially by telephone. All but two of the interviewees were recruited in person. The researcher explained the nature and significance of the study, and the privacy safeguards, and also encouraged voluntary participation. The prospective interviewees were told that their voluntary participation in the focus groups would only be needed for one hour. Post-secondary experience should be the equivalent of two semesters; therefore each subject was at least a sophomore. Moreover, respondents needed to be an Atlantica citizen, since this study purports to investigate domestic cultural relationships among individuals often identified as "Black" or "White." It was made clear that an interview time would be negotiated among the group participants. If a potential participant appeared to be European American, but denied European ancestry, claiming to be of another ancestry, that individual was considered ineligible and was not recruited to participate. Self-reported cultural affiliation ensures that the interviewee has first-hand experience with the subject matter being discussed.

Within two weeks, both sets of interviewees were identified, and a date for the focus group discussion was agreed upon. Each group was canceled once because of absences and tardiness. Six participants per college were recruited. The twelve interviewees who participated had a very high motivation level, due to the nature of the topic and its potentially cathartic effects.

The secondary study was implemented to verify the initial results from the focus group interviews. Furthermore, the secondary study examined the identity concerns of African American and European American students in a totally different region of the country (New Orleans, Louisiana). These students also attend different-race colleges (e.g., European Americans at an "Historically Black College or university," or HBCU).

A fourteen-item survey instrument was used to gather data, to answer three of the four research questions of the study. The third research question, (How does negotiation of cultural identity pose long-term identity consequences for European American and African American respondents), is not examined within the secondary study. The researcher decided that this question could best be answered open-endedly, since it required some elaboration. Using a five-point Likert scale, the respondents were presented with a series of statements, and asked to indicate the extent to which s/he agreed with each one.

The survey respondents were required to meet the first four criteria listed (See Figure 6.1). This same criteria was used to recruit participants through both convenient and randomized sampling techniques (See Figure 6.2).

In conjunction with the university registrars, faculty, or administrators, voluntary participation was encouraged. Subsequently, students referred friends

Figure 6.2
Focus Group Profiles

PU: Pacifica university

Total Number of Students:	6
Number of Females:	2
Number of Males	4
Number of Undergraduates	0
Number of Professional Students	3
Number of Graduate Students	3
Age Range:	26-45
Average # of years at PU:	3 years
Majors:	Occupational therapy, medicine

AU: Atlantica university

Total Number of Students:	6
Number of Females	5
Number of Males	1
Number of Undergraduates	5
Number of Professional Students	0
Number of Graduate Students	1
Age Range:	18-38
Average Years at AU:	3 years

Majors: International studies, public affairs, economics, accounting, marketing, undecided.

Note: In this case, professional students are those specializing in medicine or law.

Pacifica, Atlantica, Antarctica, and Arctica universities are fictititious names used to protect the reputations of those schools in which the respondents were enrolled.

who also met the criteria. Random and convenience sampling procedures were concurrently performed at both Arctica and Antarctica universities. In the case of the random sampling, the university databases were used to identify potential respondents. The school contacted the students, explained the study, and referred them to me if interested. The students were not required to contact the researcher, much less to offer their names, phone numbers, or addresses.

DESCRIPTION OF INTERVIEW RESPONDENTS

The initial study included two focus groups composed of six volunteer interviewees each. The first group from Pacifica University consisted of all European American (EA) informants, while the other group from Atlantica University had all African American (AA) informants. The age range of the participants was between 18 and 45, classified as sophomores, juniors, seniors, graduate, and professional students. The two common factors shared by participants within each group were race and university affiliation as a student.

Additionally, all participants presently live and attend school within the D.C. metropolitan area. A description of the focus groups' composition is given in Figure 6.2.

DESCRIPTION OF SURVEY RESPONDENTS

The secondary study solicited the participation of a total of thirty respondents, with equal participation from both Arctica   and Antarctica universities. In the initial study, the recruited participants were African American   undergraduate students and European American   graduate students. There was some concern about this disparity. Consequently, in the second study I recruited African American graduate students and European American undergraduate students,   to offer a balance of perspectives as it relates to educational background and perceptions of identity maturation. The age range of the respondents was deemed irrelevant for this component of the study. Among the African American   graduate respondents were six law students, four engineering students, two accounting students, one chemistry student, one education student, and one social work student.   The European American undergraduate students included ten pre-pharmacy students, two biology students, two English students, and one pre-medical student. The average years of experience was three for the undergraduate students, and two and a half for the graduate students.   Again, the two common factors among respondents from each university were race and university affiliation. Additionally, all subjects lived within the New Orleans, Louisiana metropolitan area.

SELECTION OF UNIVERSITIES

Originally, the University of Maryland and the University of the District of Columbia were target colleges for this investigation. However, as the study progressed, it appeared that Pacifica and Atlantica universities were more comparable for the focus group interviews. The percentage of minority students was relatively similar; and the total student populations were almost identical. An Institutional Review Board approval was also obtained from the University of the District of Columbia as a safeguard, in case subjects could not be recruited from Pacifica University. Moreover, both were research institutions located in

Washington, D.C.; therefore, the number of commuter students were about the same for each school.   See Figure 6.3 for the student population profiles.

Figure 6.3
Pacifica and Atlantica Universities' Student Population Profiles

Pacifica University

EA-- European American
Total Student Population: 10,719
Number of EA Students: 203
Number of EA Undergraduates: 52
Number of EA Graduate/Professional: 151
EA -- Percent of Total Population: 2

Atlantica University

AA-- African American
Total Student Population: 11,084
Number of AA Students: 801
Number of AA Undergraduates: 436
Number of Graduate/Professional: 365
AA -- Percent of Total Population: 7.2

For the survey study, Arctica and Antarctica universities were chosen. Both of these private universities have rich academic histories and diverse student bodies.

RELIABILITY AND VALIDITY OF THE INSTRUMENT

In order to achieve the measuring instrument's consistency or stability, the researcher computed Cronbach's alpha coefficients for each of the eight content areas discussed in Chapter 4. The coefficients ranged from .77 to .90 for each factor.   This particular internal consistency method was deemed most appropriate because of its ability to achieve a reliability index based upon multiple randomly selected pairs from the instrument.   A five-point Likert-type scale ranging from 1 ("agree") to 5 ("disagree") was applied to assess all eight content areas and their relationship to the investigation's research questions.   The responses from the same five students who assisted in establishing content validity were used to compute the alpha coefficients.

Before administering the instrument, I independently gathered feedback from five students (per school) with parallel sample characteristics (see Figure 6.3). This advice was sought in order to determine whether the instrument actually measured the constructs (i.e., content areas) it purported to measure.   Each of the students provided feedback regarding the labeling and structure of the content areas. It was agreed by both sets of students that the categories were rigidly and satisfactorily defined. Consequently, the investigation proceeded after satisfying the requirements associated with content validity.

SAMPLE SIZE AND GENERALIZABILITY

According to Mary John Smith (1988), an adequate sample size can be computed by using the following equation: $Nn/N + n$. The result led me to sample sizes of fifteen per population. This number represents 12 percent of the European American undergraduate student population at Arctica University (n = 123) and 5% of the African American graduate student population (n = 325) at Antarctica University.

INSTITUTIONAL REVIEW BOARD

A proposal for the use of human subjects within this investigation was presented to the Institutional Review Boards (IRB) for the Protection of Human Subjects at Pacifica, Atlantica, Arctica, and Antarctica universities. Pacifica and Atlantica approved the study in July 1995. Arctica and Antarctica approved the study in September 1995.

AUDIOTAPING

Each focus group interviewee was informed that the discussion would be audiotaped. Each was asked to sign a consent form that authorized confidential use of the interview for research purposes. The consent form was authorized by both the Pacifica University and the Atlantica University Institutional Review Boards. Participants were told that only four people would have access to the tape: the researcher and Pacifica and Atlantica University's IRBs. The consent form contained a statement promising that the tape would be demagnetized and discarded after the study was completed.

"This form [consent form] basically says that you know you are being audiotaped and that the greatest measures of confidentiality are taken -- precautionary measures." The researcher further emphasized confidentiality: "Whatever is said here in this room, I ask that you keep it here because of the confidentiality." Also, the researcher encouraged active participation. "And basically the only rules are that you can talk as much as you want about whatever you want." The one-hour discussion began with the signing of consent forms, a preamble, the protocol for discussion, and one simple question, "What's the first thing that comes to mind when someone asks you what culture you are?" At the conclusion, everyone was thanked for voluntarily participating.

RESEARCH QUESTIONS

Four research questions were created to illustrate the problem of the study. By utilizing the Third Culture Model and the Communication theory of Ethnic Identity, which structure the study, the following questions were investigated within both studies:

1. What similarities and differences were reported in the way that each of the European American and the African American students define themselves culturally?

2. What are the similarities and differences in the process of cultural identity negotiation among European American and African American students?

3. How does negotiation of cultural identity pose long-term identity consequences for European American and African American respondents?

4. Under what conditions do European American and African American respondents feel the need to reconsider their cultural identities?

The research questions were the guidelines used to construct the protocol for the focus group interviews. It is important to note that focus group researchers considered the investigator to be the "instrument." In order to understand this, an explanation follows.

FOCUS GROUPS AS TECHNIQUE

A Brief History and Explanation

While focus group interviewing is not a new data-collection technique, it is one which deserves more attention among interpretive communication researchers. Unlike surveys, which are frequently administered in accordance with quantitative communication research, the focus group has not been frequently used as a data-collection method. The focus group, Lindlof (1995) suggests, was best exemplified by the early classical studies of Robert K. Merton and Patricia Kendall (1946). Merton, Fiske, and Kendall (1956) initiated focus groups as a data-collection method while examining the persuasiveness of World War II training and propaganda films. The authors offered useful advice on the planning and execution of focus groups. Morgan (1988) explained, however, that the reason focus groups "virtually disappeared in social scientific research" (p. 11) is probably the authors' use of other methods in their published research studies. Recently though, communication scholars have utilized this technique to explore issues related to ethnic and cultural identity (Collier and Thomas, 1989; Hecht et al., 1993; Keane-Dawes, 1995; Nicotera, 1993).

Focus group interviewing was preceded by models associated with group therapy, T-groups, encounter marathons, and sensitivity training (Templeton, 1994). The setting, time, and panel size are key concerns. The facilities should be comfortable, with adequate lighting, and feasible for conversation. Templeton recommends a conference table setting for pleasant, relaxing, but still a work-related atmosphere. The best time for most employed adults is the evening, and if two groups are scheduled in one night, the author suggests that those who live the farthest from the facility be scheduled first. Panel size is another issue, which the author notes as a matter of preference. Templeton claims that investigators typically contend that groups larger than nine people afford little time for turn-taking and elaboration; nonetheless, he encourages groups of ten to twelve panelists (p. 27). Morgan (1988), on the other hand, proposed a moderate-sized group comprising six to ten respondents. He further commented that most marketing firms currently favor six to eight persons per group; anything less than four or more than twelve is not considered a focus group interview.

The interview is divided into at least six components: warm-up, introduction, preface, explanation of audio- or video-recording, recapitulation, and concluding remarks (p.28). These elements ensure a well-organized interview. The group discussion begins with an uninterrupted statement by each respondent, usually personal, followed by a lead into the questions on the interview guide. Morgan (1988) recommended that the moderator ask the interviewees to take a few minutes to prepare written notes prior to the opening statement. This acts as a deterrent to "groupthink" (Janis, 1982).

In qualitative research, interviews are used to gather firsthand information on past experiences, present interpretations, and personal descriptions of relationships, events, and overall meaning (Lindlof, 1995). Investigators using this paradigm are considered the "instrument" (Cassell, 1977; Guba and Lincoln, 1981); therefore integrity and consistency are principal aspects of the process (Lindlof, 1995). Qualitative data is rich with details of experience, captured in an in-group language. It is precisely this language which must be critically accounted for as the researcher notes patterns of association and assumption (McCracken, 1988).

McCracken discusses the notion of "self as instrument" (p. 19). The researcher becomes a necessary conduit through which data is gathered. The researcher is responsible for the level of disclosure and comfort. If the researcher's disposition seems hostile or uninviting to the respondent, the level of disclosure will decrease (Lindlof, 1995). In contrast, if the researcher is well liked, he or she may obtain greater elaboration and insight into other related issues not anticipated within the interviews (Lincoln and Guba, 1985). The researcher must maintain a "manufactured distance" (McCracken, 1988, p. 22) and also a certain "sensitivity" (Marshall and Rossman, 1989, p. 105) which afford the respondents the flexibility to express ideas and expound on social structures and systems of meaning.

The most difficult task for the rapporteur is to combine social skills, self-knowledge, and information-exploration to achieve clarification and understanding needed to interpret accurately the beliefs and ideas conveyed (McCracken, 1988; Lindlof, 1995; Templeton, 1994). These considerations capture the four objectives of the qualitative paradigm as articulated by Lincoln and Guba: credibility, transferability, dependability, and confirmability (p. 296).

Lindlof suggests that qualitative researchers employ constructs, which are often considered to have truth-value by critically assessing applicability, consistency, and neutrality. This study embraces the four objectives of Lincoln and Guba as mentioned above.

The credibility of the researcher is a reasonable concern for the interpretive critic, since the ideas of the subject(s) must be accurately reported and represented. This was accomplished in the present study as explained in Chapter 4 by shuffling and reshuffling the cards and performing several checks for accuracy to ensure authenticity of data analysis. Moreover, memo-writing serves as a useful component of the constant comparison technique. This requires a journal of decisions made during the analysis.

The transferability of technique and analysis becomes the decision of subsequent investigators, who determine whether the study's parameters are sufficiently consistent to be applied elsewhere. Two of the major parameters to be considered within the present investigation are context and culture. Therefore, a cross-situational and cross-cultural analysis must be implemented in connection with further negotiation-of-cultural-identity studies.

Dependability refers to the researcher's sensitivity to varying conditions of time, location, and overall context. Consideration of change as a natural component of the human condition is another facet of this paradigm. The researcher was forced to cancel each focus group once due to absences. The researcher's response to the extenuating circumstances and varying conditions was deemed favorable by respondents.

Confirmability is the final condition. The findings can be confirmed by future researchers only to the degree that the conditions and parameters are the same. Subjectivity must be controlled for, or the results will reflect inherent bias. Marshall and Rossman (1989, pp. 147-148) advise the following precautions: find a research partner who can play the devil's advocate and critically question interpretations; check and recheck the data for potential rival hypotheses; practice value-free note-taking; and conduct an audit of data collection and analytic strategies. This was accomplished by checking and rechecking data and negotiating differences with a trained coder.

CHAPTER SNAPSHOT

The purpose of the interpretive investigation is to discover meaning as construed by a set of cultural members. The number of individuals and their shared characteristics are secondary concerns. Meaning creation and assessment is primary; thus the research is said to be "much more intensive than extensive in its objectives" (McCracken, 1988, p. 17). Lindlof (1995) suggests six to twelve respondents per focus group. The author adds that this number is "deceptively small" (p. 32). Every word spoken by each group member during the one-hour interview must be transcribed and analyzed to extract the emergent themes and categories of response. The trends are then assessed using a data analysis technique -- in this case the Constant Comparison Technique initiated by Glaser and Strauss (1967).

Chapter 7

When "The Other" Is White: Cultural Identity and Sensemaking

> I think in order to make it in this society, in order to be prosperous, in order to raise a family, you have to be part of [the dominant culture]. . . And, I think for African Americans, they have to make changes. They have to change themselves. [statement made by a European American male student at Pacifica University].

INTRODUCTION

Chapter 7 presents the empirical findings of the present investigation. The implementation of the initial study using focus group interviews, and of the secondary study using a survey instrument, provided an added dimension to the research design. The combination of the interpretive and quantitative paradigms offers a triangulated examination of cultural identity negotiation. This chapter proceeds by first explaining Lincoln and Guba's (1985) suggested use of Glaser and Strauss' (1967) Constant Comparison Technique for focus group interviewing. The transcripts were used to identify emergent categories and themes. Furthermore, the data from the secondary study, which required the use of a questionnaire, is presented within this chapter as confirmation of the findings from the focus group interviews.

CONSTANT COMPARISON TECHNIQUE

Glaser and Strauss originally presented the constant comparison method with two intentions in mind, to develop theory and represent the functionalist paradigm. Neither of these is aligned with the primary purpose of this research. Lincoln and Guba, however, reintroduced the technique for qualitative inquiry. The carefully revised method was found most appropriate for the present study, because of the study's triangulated approach. By "unitizing and categorizing . . . units of information," (p. 344) the researcher using this technique systematically considers emergent ideas and themes.

"Unitizing" is assigning heuristic value to an idea, that is the "smallest piece of information about something that can stand by itself" (p. 345). For this study, each unit was identified and recorded on separate note cards. Each of the 100 note cards was given a code, placed at the bottom center of the card; for instance, Wht-M1 was a White male in the focus group at Pacifica University. The cards were shuffled and the process of categorization began.

Categorizing entailed several steps, which inevitably created two types of themes, emergent and research-imposed. The latter is the result of the researcher's intention to accomplish research objectives or arrive at certain conclusions. These were minimized in this research by reshuffling cards and renaming themes to reflect more accurately the content of the respondents' expressed ideas. The next step taken was to read the first card and make it the first entry in the "yet-to-be-named" (p. 347) category. Then the second card was read and was either placed with the first or assigned to a whole new category. Whether a card is grouped together or separated is decided on a "look-alike feel-alike basis" (p. 347). The authors recommend over-including cards rather than under-including, since discarded cards are least able to be recovered. The process continued until all of the cards were exhausted. The only exception was when a substantial number of cards were accumulated in one set. Lincoln and Guba recommended six to eight as a substantial accumulation. Then a provisional rule was established that characterized the "essence" (p. 347) of the cards within that set. After all of the cards were assigned to different sets, they were reviewed for inconsistencies. If a card appeared not to fit within its previously assigned set, it was reassigned to a more appropriate set or to a miscellaneous pile. Ordinarily, miscellaneous cards would be reviewed as well. However, no cards of this sort emerged, since all cards fit within the emergent categories.

The entire sets were compared with other sets to account for any overlap. There was none; however, it was possible to subsume some under others in order to reduce the number of categories and still maintain internal consistency. The rules were also reconsidered so that the propositional statement accurately portrayed the cards within the set. Finally, the cards were checked again to ascertain whether the rules and themes were appropriate. Each card containing the provisional rule was labeled with a theme meant to capture the substance of the included cards.

FINDINGS FROM THE FOCUS GROUP INTERVIEWS

The first group from Pacifica University consisted of all European American (EA) informants, while the other group from Atlantica University had all African American (AA) informants. The age range of the participants was 18-45, classified as sophomores, juniors, seniors, graduate, and professional students. The two common factors shared by participants within each group were race and university affiliation as a student. Additionally, all participants lived and attended school within the Washington D.C. metropolitan area. A description of the focus groups' composition is depicted in Figure 6.2.

This investigation required two focus groups; therefore, two different sets of themes emerged. However, the researcher organized these themes into three distinct categories to facilitate readability. Eight themes emerged from the

European American students' discussion, and five from the African American student focus group, for a total of thirteen themes. The themes are listed in Figure 7.1 subsumed under the categories, "Race and Culture, Identity" and "No Negotiation Is Necessary."

Category One: Race and Culture

As noted in Figure 7.1, category one emerged to represent "race and culture." Five themes are subsumed under this rubric. Each theme includes a provisional rule which describes the comments offered by the respondents. For example, the provisional rule for theme one states that "defining culture" addressed the respondents' understanding of their own sense of self.

Themes one through five were primarily concerned with cultural self-definition, relating specifically to the first research question in this study, which asked what similarities and differences there were in the way that European American and African American respondents define themselves culturally.

Figure 7.1
Emergent Categories and Themes

Category One: *Race and Culture*

European American Respondents
Theme One: Defining Culture
Theme Two: Just American
Theme Three: No Difference
Theme Four: Prejudice and Race relations
African American Respondents
Theme Five: Defining African American Culture

Category Two: *Identity*

European American Respondents
Theme Six: Social Adjustment
Theme Seven: No Concern for Cultural Identity
African American Respondents
Theme Eight: Causes and Effects of Cultural Identity Negotiation
Theme Nine: Necessity of Cultural Identity
Theme Ten: African American Identity and Distinctiveness

Category Three: *No Negotiation Necessary*

European American Respondents
Theme Eleven: Whites as Dominant Culture
Theme Twelve: No Negotiation of Cultural Identity
African American Respondents
Theme Thirteen: Reasons for Not Negotiating

The European American respondents, when asked to define their culture, were unable to provide a clear definition. Several of them presumed that European American culture was synonymous with American culture and were unsure how to define it. Two participants, one male and one female, explained "You can't really call it anything in particular. It's whatever you want it to be. In America you can't hardly define it." Another interviewee notes, " I'm an American, I have no culture." Similarly, a forty-five-year-old female interviewee commented: "I know I'm European-Irish. But, I know that's not really who I am. And you come here, and there are so many other people who think that that's important . . . . And with my cultural identity, I don't have any other than being American. I think that's fine. Before, I was thinking that maybe I should look more into my heritage. But, I'm an American and that's the core of it, I guess." So, while some individual respondents seem to have never contemplated the significance of a cultural self-definition, two others consciously decided to identify the undefined [in this case] American culture as their own. The other, a twenty-six-year-old Jewish student, voiced his concern: "For me, it's a little more difficult, because I'm American. I subscribe to a lot of American values and the culture. But then, being Jewish is more than just a religion. It's a culture in and of itself. And, so I have strong ties, very strong ties with that." This respondent later admitted that all American people are basically the same and defined himself as an American. Comments such as these typified the general sentiment of the European American interviewees.

Theme two, labeled "just American" included statements which examined the degree to which the participants felt the need to define themselves culturally. The participants reported that it was unnecessary and inappropriate to define one's self as anything other than American if one lives in the United States of America. One European American male accentuated this concern by noting that an American cultural identity is inescapable for those with American citizenship.

The comments contained in theme three were especially significant. This theme was labeled "no difference" and proposed the idea that African Americans and European Americans are basically the same. Two European American males and two European American females revealed their opinions regarding prejudice and assimilation: "It doesn't matter if I come up to a person. I try to look at them as an individual, and try not to see them with any prejudice, but it's hard, because it's ingrained in . . . our culture. . . . Here, you know, eventually you do become color blind. Very much so, being here, I have. I'm sure many of you have as well. . . . If you're not interacting within a group of people, you tend to homogenize them. And, you know, it's just a natural thing."

These comments reflect the attitudes presented within the interview, which relate to racial homogeneity. The statement "We're all basically the same" was repeated several times by at least three respondents -- two males and one female. The other three nodded their heads in agreement. The feedback received from the six interviewees clearly indicated a shared perception among them that there was no need to define themselves culturally and that there is only one basic culture in America. An interesting statement that testifies to this opinion was offered by the self-identified American-Jewish male participant who explained that there may be Asians, Hispanics, and "Blacks," but ultimately our cultures are all meshed together and "pre-negotiated." This feeling of an inevitable American culture that consumes all nationalities and citizenships disengages the process of Third Culture Building. The third-culture building exchange requires interactants from both cultures to begin to question, reconsider, and relinquish a portion of their cultural identities. That portion identified by Starosta and Olorunnisola (Chen and Starosta, 1998) is composed of values, mores and attitudes. According to the authors, without "responding to the symbolic realities of another entity that has been differentially socialized" (p. 212), the Third Culture Building model can not progress. The statements of theme three are significant because of the commentary relating to homogeneity. If one believes that two cultures are the same, there are no grounds for negotiation, since individuals only seek to negotiate when they can acquire something different from what they already have.

Theme four, "prejudice and race relations," involves concerns of racial prejudice and stereotyping. A European American male participant reported that he had previously attended a predominantly White institution in Harrisburg, Virginia, where Blacks were only 10 percent of the population. He contrasted this experience with the experience he has had at Pacifica University, and concluded that he had developed several preconceived notions about African Americans while in Virginia. Now, he was surprised to find more similarities than differences in the two cultures.

All of the respondents revealed that they had gained some "insight" into how African Americans really are. They mentioned how their perceptions had been formed by how the news portrays African Americans as violent criminals, suspect murderers, and lazy, intellectually inferior beings. A male interviewee reported that he expected to see Black males in handcuffs. Two European American male students of Pacifica University reminisced about how frightened they had been to walk to Taco Bell at lunchtime. They had been afraid of getting robbed, mugged, and beaten, so they always walked in groups to get lunch. Even after they became more comfortable, they noticed other fearful European American males walking close to them as they walked to the "strip" alone.

The forty-five-year-old European American female interviewee stated that she did not see much difference between being a Pacifica University student and an employee in XYZ corporation. She explained that it was just a different set of people with their own distinct differences. Another female respondent rationalized that there probably are more differences than similarities, but because of the academic context, everyone seems so similar. The concern for race relations was more of an interest in learning the similarities and differences between the behaviors of European Americans and African Americans.

African American respondents from Atlantica University were also asked to define their culture (theme five: "defining African American culture"). In a focus group interview separate from the European American subjects, these students confided that African American culture is distinct. It has been shaped and defined, according to these students, by struggle, musical variety, African descent, and matriarchal family structure. The struggle was described by one African American female participant as "trying to achieve something that was taken." Another African American female participant describes struggle as the "rape that occurred when our ancestors were. . . forced to come over here. And African Americans are unique because for so long we have been brainwashed . . . ashamed of who we are and what we are. . . . [The struggle describes] things that we've had to endure here [in America]." Another African American female respondent identified adaptability as a characteristic of African American culture. She expressed her belief that African Americans are among the few living peoples who can proudly say "even after we were totally removed from our society, we still survived." She further suggested that although struggle is part of the culture, African Americans can overcome any struggle.

The second distinctive element of African American culture is musical variety; The respondents asserted that jazz, blues, rap, and gospel music indicate the varied music listening preferences within the community. The music genres are only one symbol of the diversity found among African Americans.

A third element is African descent. When asked to discuss her cultural identity, a thirty-six-year-old African American female participant explained that she identified herself as Black; being Black, she says, suggests that Native Africans, Trinidadians, African Americans, and other African descendants all share the same cultural origin. Yet, each culture has been distinctly developed. She commented that many African Americans perceive a disconnectedness with African culture because they have never lived or even visited there. However, she explained, "If people look at you, and you may have a darker tone to your skin. Immediately, they're not going to ask you if you're African or if you're from Trinidad, they're going to say that you're Black and assume that you're African American. That forces you to develop your own [cultural identity]." Finally, the fourth distinctive element is a matriarchal family structure, which was described as being typical of African diasporic societies and African American culture. The six focus group respondents agreed upon these four distinctions and revealed a definite concern for cultural self-definition.

Category Two: Identity

Themes six through ten address issues related to cultural identity. In theme six, "social adjustment," European American students reported having learned several things matriculating and adjusting at Pacifica University -- social behaviors and practices such as handshaking, slang-talking, and dancing. When asked if they had ever reconsidered the exchange of their own cultural values, attitudes, and beliefs for that of another, one European American female exclaimed, "I don't have time." Later in the interview, the question was presented again, and another female respondent stated that she would be open to this exchange, since she has a sociology background and all different societies interest her. However, she completed this sentence by saying, "I think I'm who I am, and I don't want to change that." European American students implied that exploration of cultural identity is an activity reserved for undergraduates and those who have leisure time. The major adjustments these students feel they have encountered include social practices.

Handshaking was described by an European American male as being difficult, since he feels he would be perceived as imitating African Americans. In particular, the "soul" handshake was being discussed. The respondents spent approximately fifteen minutes sharing different experiences with handshaking behavior. Part of the discussion between two European American males went as follows:

I know how to do. . . . the handshake or whatever . . . . But, I feel like I may be looking like, "Who is this, you know, stupid White guy trying to shake h a n d s , my hand, like a Black guy." So, I kinda feel like, you know, that's one sort of barrier that I have. I'm getting closer, but. Like this I can do, the fist ["hitting the rock" or pounding one fist on top of another].   That's sort of a strange thing for me right now. . . . I don't want to be too demonstrative../Well then don't do it. /I don't and I don't, but. . . . I'm getting to the point right now where I am comfortable with it.

Of particular significance in this discussion is the response by another interviewee, who discouraged his colleague from participating in the social adjustment if he was not comfortable. This, of course, presumes that imitation of the handshaking behavior of African Americans is an unnecessary option.

Another adjustment is slang-talking. When the subjects were asked if they had ever questioned their own values, beliefs, and attitudes, and attempted to adjust their behaviors to better resemble African American behavior more closely, they replied by saying, "No."   One European American male respondent confided that he was afraid he might be at a family gathering and do something that would resemble a typical African American behavior. He describes it best: "You know, it'll hit me, and I'll be like oh yeah, gee . . . it's rubbing off on me." One of the other European American male respondents reported that he might have picked up on some language or speech behaviors. When asked for a couple of examples, three interviewees, one female and two males, simultaneously responded, "Slang." No one was able to produce any examples.

A final adjustment experienced by all but the eldest European American participant, was dancing. The dances with which they had previously been familiar were much different than the Pacifica dances. Everyone excitedly revealed that they had markedly improved their dancing abilities and that they were made to feel comfortable at the dances. One male respondent even boasted that he had frequented several local nightclubs with his African American friends using the latest dance techniques. The data received within this theme revealed leisurely participation in behaviorally altering activities.

Theme seven, labeled "no concern for cultural identity," addressed the rationale that the respondents' graduate.professional student status exempts them from cultural identity exploration. Identity is depicted as a secondary concern for the European American respondents. There were three reasons given for this exemption: time, classification, and age.

"You're already in a medical situation. Your mind has to be focused on that, and then the social aspect comes second." This statement asserted by an European American male resembles another comment made by an European American female respondent who plainly admitted that she had no time to be concerned about cultural identity, since she is a mother, wife, employee, and student. As part of her justification, she mentioned that she is an older student returning to school to complete a professional degree. Consequently, because of the lack of leisure time, classification, and age, she exempted herself from being preoccupied with issues of cultural identity.   The other respondents subsequently agreed that age and student status were factors affecting their opinions about cultural identity. One female participant indicated that because they were all older students they were more established in their identities. The students further recommended that I solicit the opinions of undergraduate students who presumably would be less concerned about time and less established in their identities because of their classifications and ages.

The African American students at Atlantica University readily understood what the negotiation of cultural identity is. While they maintained that they were not presently engaging in the process, they were able to provide the "causes and effects of cultural identity negotiation" (theme eight), "the necessity of having a defined cultural identity" (theme nine) and the importance of "African American identity and distinctiveness" (theme ten).

Theme eight addresses how the negotiation of cultural identity is characterized, and also several underlying reasons why African Americans negotiate their cultural identities. The African American respondents reported that the process of cultural identity negotiation is psychological, behavioral, and physical. Two African American female subjects characterized the beginning of the process psychologically as that point when one begins questioning him or herself. The two female respondent hypothesize, "They have to personally be embarrassed. Yeah, the minute they question who they are and they'd be embarrassed about who they are, not accept who they are and then look towards another culture to find who they are." The behavioral manifestation of the negotiation is described as being linked to an individual's willingness to concede his.her worldview by allowing "White people to dominate every aspect." Another female student indicated her belief that people who alter their behavior around "White people" are insecure in themselves. According to another female respondent, this is often portrayed in African Americans' decisions to alter their physical appearances. The alteration of the nose was one example of this.

The underlying reasons for negotiating cultural identity offered by the African American interviewees at Atlantica University were as follows: needing to belong, nurturance and family advice, material gain, self-hatred, insecurity, poor self-esteem, and the belief that "White is right." The students suggested that some African Americans who come to that large metropolitan campus feel overwhelmed, lonely, and a need to fit in with the European American students; therefore, they seek their acceptance. This seems to make the adjustment easier, since the individual feels attached to the majority culture there. Another reason given was that some students may have been taught by their families to believe that they should seek the acceptance of "Whites." Still, others may desire rank, position, or some other material gain. All of the respondents shared the opinion that self-hatred, insecurity, and poor self-esteem were common traits of a cultural identity negotiant. Finally, an African American female participant commented that some negotiants might simply believe that "White is right . . . where anything that White people do, anything that White people say, anything they wear, the parties they go to is the better way."

The effects of negotiating cultural identity that were described are depression, loss of respect, and loss of integrity. A female respondent indicated that negotiants are often unhappy with their lives. She stated that there are some cases where the person walks around with his or her head down, unable to look others in the eye. The negotiant was also characterized as having lost respect and integrity for him or herself. The ultimate consequence was revealed by a female respondent who stated, "Well, if you keep on changing yourself for other people, after a while you won't know who you are. . . . And those people that you're trying to be like will not respect you. . . . They'll see right through it."

Theme nine, labeled "necessity of cultural identity," addressed the need to have a cultural identity firmly established. Several statements were made at the beginning of the focus group interview referring to the importance of having an intact cultural identity. One female respondent commented, "I think you have to have a cultural identity in general just so you know who you are and where you come from, and where it is that you may go, or where you have the destiny to go. And, of course here at American, you have to have some sort of cultural identity, but you have to get it before you come here 'cause you'll get lost in a lot of things here." The subjects tended to agree that there are many cultures represented at Atlantica University, and many individuals remain among their own people. This is believed to be a primary reason for having a strong cultural identity at Atlantica University. A female student shared her reason for developing and maintaining an intact cultural identity. "But, on AU's campus,you definitely have to have one, because people will challenge who you are and you really have to accept who you are as a person in society. And you're not going to be accepted by anybody else but your own."

A male respondent, an athlete in his sophomore year, suggested that a grounded cultural identity is significant because, his experience dictated that "White" people often presume "Black" males are stupid or only athletes. He suggested that even within the past year his cultural identity had been strengthened. Other respondents also reported having enhanced their cultural identities since being at Atlantica University. According to the participants, this growth is due to the constant challenges of other students whose racist opinions encouraged a further examination of their self-definitions. The comments within this theme testify to the need to define self in relationship to culture.

Theme ten, "African American Identity and Distinctiveness," addresses the nature and distinctiveness of African American identity. When asked to define their cultural membership, the African American respondents immediately claimed to be "Black" and "African American." Two students indicated that African American culture preserves its distinctiveness primarily through struggle. In other words, the interviewees suggested they had been forced to think about who they are. The predicament of African Americans was said to be distinctive for several reasons: the attempted "brainwashing" by European Americans in the early 1600s; ignorance of a specific national or cultural ancestry; geographic location; and socio-cultural milieux.

The attempted erasure of culture during the Middle Passage is but one of the prominent distinctions of the culture. Many African Americans still do not know much about African culture. Specifically, most African Americans may find it difficult to trace their lineage to a particular country within the continent of Africa. Another distinction is the geographic location of African Americans. These African descendants are still within the context of the United States, which has certain cultural traditions of its own. Finally, the socio-cultural milieux was said to refer to the experiences that African Americans endure on a daily basis due to skin color and cultural heritage. These aspects of African

American cultural distinctiveness provide a capsule for understanding the importance of cultural identity development among the African American students.

Category Three: No Negotiation Necessary

Category three comprises the rationales given by both the European American and African American students, for not negotiating cultural identity. The European American students' comments are reflected within themes eleven ("Whites As Dominant Culture") and twelve ("No Negotiation of Cultural Identity"). The African American students' comments are provided within theme thirteen ("Reasons for Not Negotiating").

Theme eleven, labeled "whites as dominant culture," addressed the fact that European American students are part of the dominant culture and the effects that that has had on their Pacifica University experiences. An interesting aspect of the discussion about being European Americans at an HBCU unfolded intensely among five of the participants:

I have to say that negotiating cultural identity is kind of a vague term and I don't really think it applies in any situation. I don't think you're ever negotiating your cultural identity. . . . it's easy for us to say that because whatever culture we have as European White Americans, we are the dominant culture in this society. . . . who has the most power . . . . How much does that trickle down into my everyday life? I think a lot of it does. . . Probably more than you recognize.

A male respondent reported his belief that African American students were having a difficult time adjusting to his presence as a student at Pacifica. He, as well as two other students (one male, one female), revealed having been confronted with degrading comments by professors and students. Professors, for example, would say certain things like, "Good White folk, or in this instance White means good" to typecast European Americans. The same male participant that reported these comments stated that a professor even told him, "All you White boys look alike." This type of resistance led one male respondent to the conclusion that all people are prejudice no matter what culture is claimed.

When asked if they thought they had to make changes, one European American male respondent said that he was already in the mainstream, which is where everyone should be if they are to be successful. Particularly, he identified African Americans, Asians, and Latinos as just a few examples of those who "have to change themselves." Another European American male indicated that when he arrives at Pacifica for classes, he doesn't feel like he's in the dominant culture but when he leaves campus he feels, "I'm back in it. I'm accepted. I'm a part of it. It's ingrained in me." The comments continued to suggest that the respondents come to campus and interact, but their behaviors do not change. They even doubted that any change in behavior existed among African American students at a university composed mostly of European Americans.

Theme twelve, labeled "No Negotiation of Cultural Identity," addressed the respondents' lack of cultural identity negotiation. Several of the students interviewed implied that there had been no apparent changes in the way that they behave or communicate. One female student mentioned that it was possible the alterations were subconscious, but she was not conscious of undergoing any changes. Another female participant inquired whether culture is hereditary. One reason given by the older female respondent for not negotiating cultural identity is that she felt competent enough to successfully thrive in "different situations." She expressed her uncertainty as to how someone could alter their cultural identity.

Comments within this theme clearly supported the notion that cultural identity negotiation is not experienced by at least these European American students, even after being exposed to a different cultural context.

Theme thirteen, labeled "reasons for not negotiating" addressed the African American students' resistance to negotiating cultural identity at a predominantly European American institution.

When asked if there had ever been a time when they found themselves altering their behaviors when interacting with European Americans, the African American students responded: "Hell no, I don't change a thing for anybody... No. No, no, no, no, because . . . . You cannot negotiate who you are for these people here, because if you don't stand up for something, then they damn sure not going to stand up for you, and then if you . . . kinda waiver on your decision, then they're going to take it as everyone else is going to waiver on their decisions, and they're going to think they can walk all over you." Subsequent comments revealed that African Americans had already negotiated enough throughout the years. Several reasons surfaced for not negotiating cultural identity. They were as follows: integration has not helped; color blindness is a problem; there is no need to "uncle-tom"; there is no need for "White" acceptance; and, the African American race must progress.

An African American female respondent expressed the concern that integration has not helped. "They just want you to totally give up your Blackness. . . . We better get off this we-are-the-world-kick," she exclaimed. Other students offered instances of how African Americans have been discriminated against regardless of integration. One example referred to African American students at Atlantica University whose financial aid mysteriously disappeared. Every semester, the participants said, this occurs, and it seems to be aimed specifically at the African American students.

The second reason for not negotiating is the problems associated with color-blindness. The students concluded that European Americans espouse the doctrine of color blindness to promote assimilation. Color blindness was defined as ignoring skin color; however, a female respondent asked, "How can you do that?" Another female respondent explained that this was called Uncle-Tomming.

The third reason reported for not negotiating cultural identity is that there is no longer a need for Uncle-Tomming. The participants discussed the fact that uncle-tomming was done to "get ahead," but according to three female students, present socioeconomic conditions allow African Americans to begin appreciating, understanding, and maintaining their cultural heritage.

The fourth reason is that there is no need to seek "White people's" acceptance. The eldest African American female respondent confided that she was familiar with several other African Americans who wanted to be a part of the "White country clubs," but she felt as though that this was unnecessary. Her concern was that it resembled integration.

Finally, the general comments presented suggested a shared concern that because the "Black race" needs to progress, negotiating cultural identity would be detrimental. The resultant effects are best described by two of the female respondents:

The whole race takes a step backwards if you compromise . . . . and we'll never go forward, in believing in ourselves as a people. We need to get back into the village and each one, teach one. . . I think if you start to or continue to compromise. . . they'll decide to pick us up and take us somewhere else. And we'll just go back from slavery. . . .Right now is such a delicate time that we're in, too. Most Black people are starting now to be just proud of the Black, proud of the dark skin and the hair. And if there's one little deviation, it could easily go right back to where it started. Because right now, it's right at that transition where people are starting to go all the way to accepting themselves, and once people are accepting of themselves, that's the only way people can accept you.

The reported comments within theme thirteen provide some insight into the rationale behind the African American students not feeling the need to negotiate their cultural identities. The reasons given by these students were in stark contrast to those given by the European American students.

FINDINGS FROM THE SECONDARY STUDY

The research team for this investigation found it necessary to further examine the notion of cultural identity negotiation among a different population of students. The idea was initiated to provide verification of the results from the focus group interviews. There were three benefits of implementing the secondary study: to offer a balance of the graduate and undergraduate experiences across cultural boundaries; to discover whether the same results would be achieved outside of the vicinity of the Eastern Coast of the United States; and to learn whether the quantitative approach would yield similar results.

The secondary study included fifteen students each from Arctica and Antarctica universities (New Orleans, Louisiana). The opinions of European American graduate students and African American undergraduate students had already been examined at Pacifica and Atlantica universities (Washington, D.C.), respectively. Consequently, in order to offer a balance, in terms of academic classification, of the different cultural experiences, the unexamined populations were investigated. In other words, European American undergraduate students and African American graduate students were conveniently sampled at Arctica and Antarctica universities , respectively. The first statement of the survey asked if the respondents agreed with the idea that graduate students negotiate identity just as much as undergraduate students. Both sample populations reported agreement with the statement.

The data revealed a positive verification of the results from the focus group interviews: the same results were achieved outside of the vicinity of Washington, D.C., and were arrived at using a quantitative approach.

A fourteen-item survey instrument was used to gather data, which would answer three of the four research questions of the study. The third research question (How does negotiation of cultural identity pose long-term identity consequences for European American and African American respondents) was not examined in the secondary study. The researcher decided that this question could best be answered open-endedly, since it requires some elaboration. Using a five-point Likert scale, the respondents were presented with a series of statements, and asked to indicate the extent to which she agreed with each one.

Although each subject was given a fourteen-item questionnaire, eight statistical tests needed to be executed in order to analyze the collected data. Each test required a content-area label that described the construct being measured. Five t tests and three z tests were computed. Each of the sample population means, as well as the derived t and z scores are given in Table 7.1.

According to Mary John Smith (1988), a noted quantitative research scholar, the t test is most appropriately applied when an investigator is assessing the significance of mean differences among sample sizes comprising fewer than thirty scores. If the sample size is thirty scores or greater, then a z test is recommended. These two suggestions were employed when I determined the statistical technique to be used for the two sample populations examined in the present study.

The eight content areas were analyzed in accordance with concerns raised from the initial study as well as research questions 1, 2, and 4, which relate to cultural self-definition, the process of negotiating cultural identity (NCI), and conditions motivating negotiation, respectively. Each content area has been labeled to identify better the fourteen Likert-type survey questions (SQ's) each of which examined a certain aspect of NCI.

The eight areas are: cultural self-definition (SQ #2; a =.90), ancestral heritage (SQ #3; a = .87), process of NCI (SQ's 6, 8, 10, 12, 13, 14; a = .77), codeswitching (SQ's 4 and 5; a = .85) , the benefits of NCI (SQ #8; a = .83), the hazards of NCI (SQ #9; a = .85), conditions motivating NCI (SQ's 7 and 11; a = .67) and negotiation based upon classification (SQ #1; a = .87). Cronbach's alpha coefficients ranged from .77 to .90 for each factor; a five-point scale (ranging from "disagree to agree") was applied to assess all of the content areas. Aside from using factor analysis and Cronbach's alpha tests to find variable groupings and scale reliability, the statistical significance for all tests was set at the .01 level. All except three content areas were statistically significant. An explanation of each content area and the results from each are discussed.

The first two content areas are cultural self-definition and ancestral heritage, both of which relate to the first research question of the study, which asks: What similarities and differences were reported in the way that European American and African American students defined themselves culturally? "Cultural self-definition" is the label given to describe responses to the statement declaring that the respondent's culture is the same as American culture. Arctica and Antarctica University students differed significantly (t = 3.64, p < .01) in their tendency to equate their cultures with American culture. African American students from Antarctica University were almost in complete agreement regarding this notion of the distinctiveness of African American culture.

The second content area is ancestral heritage, which refers to the respondents' need to define themselves on the basis of their cultural ancestry. The African American students felt a much greater need to define themselves on the basis of their ancestral heritage than did the European American students.

Table 7.1
Mean Scores for Survey Content Areas

Content Area	n	Mean score	Derived t score	Derived z score
European American Students				
Arctica University				
Cultural Self-definition	15	3.60		
Ancestral Heritage	15	4.30	3.64	
Process of NCI	90	3.70	6.32	1.00
Codeswitching	30	4.00		5.31
Benefits of NCI	15	3.87	5.10	
Hazards of NCI	15	3.60	3.02	
Conditions Motivating NCI	30	4.00		.61
Negotiation Based on Classification	15	2.47	1.00	
African American Students				
Antarctica University				
Cultural Self-definition	15	4.80		
Ancestral Heritage	15	1.90	3.64	
Process of NCI	90	3.50	6.32	1.00
Codeswitching	30	2.30		5.31
Benefits of NCI	15	2.80	5.10	
Hazards of NCI	15	2.30	3.02	
Conditions Motivating NCI	30	4.20		.61
Negotiation Based on Classification	15	2.87	1.00	

NOTE: NCI = Negotiation of Cultural Identity

The two population means varied greatly, and the result of the analysis also indicated that the difference was statistically significant ($t = 6.32$, $p < .01$).

The third content area, "the process of Negotiation of Cultural Identity (NCI)," was the largest computation, including 180 scores and requiring the use of a z test for mean differences. Questions in this area were designed to answer the second research question which asks: what are the similarities and differences in the process of cultural identity negotiation among European American and African American college students? The results ($z = 1.00$, $p < .01$) indicated that there was no statistical significance of mean differences between Arctica and Antarctica students. This was expected, since the initial study yielded results that suggested that neither African American nor European American students felt as though they negotiated cultural identity. However in the initial study, African American students were much more cognizant of codeswitching, as well as of the benefits and hazards of NCI than European American students.

The next three content areas cover codeswitching, and the benefits and hazards of NCI. It is important to note that question 8 was examined twice. By isolating this question and conducting a separate analysis, I was better able to draw comparisons in responses to questions 8 and 9.

Arctica and Antarctica University students significantly differed in the expected direction ($z = 5.31$, $p < 01$) with regards to their reports of codeswitching behaviors. The African American students at Antarctica University clearly admitted to behavioral and communicative codeswitching behaviors. On the other hand, European American students at Arctica University did not reveal similar experiences with confronting codeswitching situations. Consequently, the conclusion drawn is that although neither group reports NCI, African Americans are familiar with the behaviors associated with this phenomenon.

Two other content areas examined whether NCI was seen as beneficial, hazardous, or both. The responses given indicated that the African American students at Antarctica University considered NCI to be both beneficial and hazardous. However, there was a significant statistical difference between the mean responses of the two groups in both of these areas - benefits ($t = 5.10$, $p < 01$)) and hazards ($t = 3.02$, $p < .01$). The mean scores of the European American students at Arctica University imply negative opinions regarding the benefits and hazards of NCI. Perhaps, the reason for this awkward consistency of response is that they felt they had never had the opportunity to experience NCI.

The conditions motivating NCI were also examined within this quantitative study. The statements that parallel this seventh content area refer to the respondents feeling pressured to redefine their cultural identities and question their cultural beliefs and values. There was no statistical significance of difference ($z = .61$, $p < .01$) between the responses of the two groups. Again, because neither group reported present NCI, they were less likely to suggest that there were conditions which motivated them to negotiate their cultural identities.

Finally, one of the concerns in the focus group study was whether graduate students negotiated cultural identity as much as undergraduate students. When presented as an affirmative statement, that graduate students do negotiate identity just as much as undergraduate students, the results yielded no statistical significance of difference ($t = 1.00$, $p < .01$). Both sets of respondents agreed that graduate students negotiated cultural identity just as much as undergraduate students. Table 7.2 illustrates the survey responses from Arctica and Antarctica

University students.

Discussion of Response Averages

The greatest disparity in response averages between the two groups was found in questions 3, 5, and 12, which addressed issues of cultural self-definition, codeswitching, and the value of cultural identity, respectively. As shown in Table 7.2, the response average for number three was 4.3 for Arctica

Table 7.2
Survey Responses from Arctica and
Anartica University Students

	Statement	ARU Students	ANU Students	# of 1s ARU/ANU	# of 5s ARU/ANU
1	Graduate students negotiate cultural identity just as much as undergraduate students.	2.47	2.87	4 / 3	0 / 2
2	AA/EA culture is the same as American culture.	3.60	4.80	1 / 0	4 / 12
3	I feel the need to define myself on the basis of my ancestral heritage.	4.30	1.90	0 / 6	8 / 0
4	I act differently with EA than I do with AA.	3.93	2.70	0 / 2	7 / 1
5	I communicate differently with EA than I do with AA.	4.00	2.00	0 / 6	7 / 1
6	At school I feel pressure to redefine my cultural identity.	4.47	3.27	0 / 2	11 / 4
7	Here at school, AA/EA are also pressured to redefine their cultural identities.	3.40	4.13	2 / 0	4 / 9
8	I see benefits in negotiating my cultural identity.	3.87	2.80	1 / 2	6 / 2
9	I see hazards in negotiating my cultural identity.	3.60	2.27	1 / 5	4 / 1
10	To me, it is acceptable to permanently alter my cultural identity.	4.60	4.73	0 / 1	11 / 14
11	Being around AA/EA causes me to question my own beliefs and values.	4.60	4.20	0 / 1	11 / 11
12	I feel that my cultural identity is valued just as much as the cultural identity of AA/EA.	2.47	4.00	6 / 2	2 / 9
13	EA/AA on this campus are concerned about changing their culutral identities.	3.70	2.80	1 / 0	6 / 1
14	AA/EA need to negotiate their cultural identities to be successful.	3.40	3.26	2 / 3	6 / 5

NOTE: EA=European Americans; AA=African Americans
        ARU=Arctica University; ANU=Anarctica University

This table shows comparisons using a Likert-type scale
from agree to disagree, with 1 being "mostly agree" and
5 being "mostly disagree."

students and 1.9 for Antarctica students, suggesting that European American students at Arctica University almost unanimously agreed that they did not need to define themselves on the basis of their ancestral heritage. Naturally, this is contingent upon the type of students with whom one interacts.

While African American students at Antarctica University clearly agreed that cultural ancestry was a viable factor in their self-definition, European American students did not seem to be as preoccupied with their cultural ancestries. Another large disparity in response rates was on statement number five, "I communicate differently with European Americans than I do with African Americans." Arctica University students disagreed with the statement, supporting the notion that they do not codeswitch their communicative behaviors. Antarctica University students agreed, expressing the essence of their experience.

The last of the recognizably large disparities in responses was on statement number 12, which expressed the degree to which the individuals feel that their cultural identities were valued in comparison to the "other" culture. Arctica students confidently reported the positive value of their cultural identities in comparison to African Americans'. However, African American respondents disagreed with the statement, indicating that their feeling that their cultural identities were not as valued. These were three of the largest disparities, but other figures from Table 7.2 are noteworthy.

Two noteworthy consistencies in response between the two sample populations occurred in questions 10, 11, and 14. Table 7.2 indicates that both groups clearly disagreed on the acceptability of permanently altering their cultural identities. Additionally, neither group felt as though their educational context forced them to question their beliefs and values. Statement 10 suggests that permanently altering cultural identity is acceptable; both groups indicated almost unanimous disagreement with this statement. This verifies the initial study which proposes that neither group negotiates cultural identity. Statement 11 questioned whether being around the other culture encourages second-guessing of one's own values and beliefs; the two groups, again, reported strong disagreement with this idea. To agree with this statement would be virtually to admit to negotiating cultural identity. Neither group admitted to cultural identity negotiation. The final statement (#14) asked the respondents if their own cultural members needed to negotiate their cultural identities to be successful. Both groups responded with uncertainty. It could be that the statement was not understood. Or, these could be authentic responses indicating a sense of indecisiveness as to the relationship between success and cultural identity negotiation.

The third and fourth columns of the table report the frequency with which the subjects responded with extreme answers. Obviously this is significant because it indicates the strength of the opinions. The opinions were considered strongest when the number of extreme responses was eight or above. This was true for questions 2, 3, 6, 7, 10, and 11.

Statement number two sought to gather opinions regarding whether the respondent considered his/her culture to be the same as American culture. As shown in Table 7.2, twelve African American respondents reported that their culture was distinctly different from American culture.

Statement number three referred to the need to define oneself on the basis of cultural ancestry. Eight European American subjects from Arctica revealed that a cultural self-definition based on ancestral heritage was completely unnecessary.

Feeling pressure to redefine one's cultural self-definition was the theme of statement six. Almost all (n = 11) of the European American respondents indicated that they experienced no pressure to redefine their cultural worldview.

Ironically, nine African American students at Antarctica predicted in statement seven that European Americans at Antarctica would not feel the pressure to redefine their cultural identities.

Aside from computing t and z scores for statistical significance of difference, I was able, by noting the apparent similarities and differences in the responses from each sample population, to determine partially whether the reported data verified the results of the initial study. Also, since the research questions were considered when designing the survey instrument, the investigation required that the survey responses also be considered when answering the study's research questions. The research questions covered four issues: cultural self-definition, the cultural identity negotiation process, long-term identity consequences, and conditions for reconsidering cultural identity.

Questions two and three were designed to provide an answer to the first research question, which asked what similarities and differences are reported in the way that the two populations define themselves culturally. No similarities were reported in the two populations' cultural self-definitions; however, there were differences. Eighty percent (n = 12) of the African American respondents indicated a strong belief that their culture was distinct from American culture. In contrast, 27 percent (n = 4) of the European American respondents reported similar opinions.

Most of the questions (#'s 4, 5, 6, 7, 8, 11, 12) were designed to gather data related to the process of cultural identity negotiation. The African American focus group interviewees at Atlantica University suggested that the process begins when one begins to question one's own values and beliefs. In response to question eleven, 73 percent (n = 11) of both sample populations reported a strong disagreement to the idea that they had felt pressure to question their cultural identities. This lack of questioning cultural self-definition verifies the findings from the focus group study, which revealed that the process is impeded by unwillingness to negotiate or reconsider their cultural identities. Starosta and Olorunnisola's (Chen and Starosta, 1998) Third Culture Building model is also prevented from moving forward at this point. Also, these survey questions verified additional focus group results, which are as follows: European American students do not feel the need to behaviorally or communicatively codeswitch; European Americans are not pressured to redefine their cultural identities; European Americans are less likely to negotiate (see Table 7.2, statement 8); and, neither population is willing to negotiate its cultural identities.

The third research question referred to long-term identity consequences. As with the focus groups, neither group was willing to begin the process of cultural identity negotiation; therefore there are no long-term identity consequences (see Table 7.2, statement 10).

The final research question relates to conditions motivating cultural identity negotiation. Statements thirteen and fourteen of the survey were designed to provide additional data which would assist in answering this question. According to the response averages illustrated in Table 7.2, African American respondents reported that changing cultural identities was at least a concern among African American students, overall, at Antarctica University. However, they were uncertain whether this same concern was being confronted by European American students.

CHAPTER SNAPSHOT

Overall, the secondary study confirms the findings of the initial focus group interviews. The implementation of the constant comparison method to analyze and interpret the focus group interviews, at Pacifica and Atlantica universities provided a grounded technique for arriving at the results from a thick-descriptivist perspective. The rich amount of data received answered each of the research questions sufficiently and helped to support the data received from the survey instrument distributed at Arctica and Antarctica universities. Consequently, the triangulated approach was successful in verifying the strength of the results from two different perspectives.

Chapter 8

The Results and Synthesis

Only once have I been made mute. It was when a man asked me, who are
you? (Gibran, 1926, p. 2)

OVERVIEW

This chapter primarily interprets the findings offered in Chapter 4, discusses
the implications, and considers future directions for research. Additionally, a
review of chapters 1-7 is given; also the problems and limitations of the present
study are reviewed, followed by concluding statements.

REVIEW OF THE PURPOSE AND
OBJECTIVES OF THE RESEARCH

The purpose of the present study was to examine systematically the process
and definition of cultural identity negotiation among students in culturally
varied educational contexts. The objectives were as follows:

1. To gather, analyze, and describe data regarding the relational aspects of
    cultural identity negotiation.

2. To identify factors influencing cultural identity negotiation.

3. To explore the extent to which African Americans and European Americans
    need to define themselves culturally.

4. To indicate any differences in the process of cultural identity negotiation
    among both cultures.

5. To analyze data received discussing consequences, motivations, and
    the duration of cultural identity negotiation.

REVIEW OF THE LITERATURE

Hecht, Collier and Ribeau were the first authors within the communication discipline to provide a thorough treatment of identity as a communicated phenomenon. Communication scholars Starosta and Olorunnisola (Chen and Starosta, 1998) created a Third Culture Model, which extends negotiation research to interpersonal and intrapersonal discourse. Yet there is still a void in the current literature on the nature and significance of cultural identity negotiation as an interacted process.

Much of the identity literature is found within the disciplines of psychology, sociology, and anthropology. Included among the various types of identity are cultural, personal, social, intergroup, ethnolinguistic, racial, and ethnic. There is a dearth of communication research concerning identity, specifically cultural identity. Hecht, Collier, and Ribeau empirically and extensively consider ethnic identity from a communication perspective.

Race, ethnicity, and culture are terms often used interchangeably; however, they have historically been defined, and continue to be described, as different constructs. Race has been identified as a biologically related characteristic. Ethnicity is considered to be a socially derived phenomenon often related to language, nationality, religion, or culinary practices. Culture, however, is defined as a process of historically transmitted symbols, beliefs, institutions, behaviors, customs, and practices. These are shared and perpetuated by a consolidated group of individuals connected by an ancestral heritage and geographical reference location. Psychologists and sociologists have most notably contributed to racial identity literature. Sociologists and communication scholars have been particularly instrumental in the development of ethnic identity research. Anthropologists and psychologists have given heuristic value to cultural identity literature. But communication scholars have only implied through intercultural research the significance and depth inherent within cultural identity investigations. If it is true that one cannot *not* communicate, then identity must be an inherent and perpetual process untapped by many communication researchers. The present study offers a critical-interpretive examination of cultural identity as an ongoing negotiation process.

REVIEW OF THE RESEARCH QUESTIONS

1. What similarities and differences were reported in the way that European American and African American students define themselves culturally?

2. What are the similarities and differences in the process of cultural identity negotiation among European American and African American students?

3. How does negotiation of cultural identity pose long-term identity consequences for European American and African American respondents?

4. Under what conditions do European American and African American respondents feel the need to reconsider their cultural identities?

REVIEW OF THE METHODS

The subjects used in the initial study were European American graduate students from Pacifica University and African American undergraduate students from Atlantica University. The secondary study involved the design and administration of a fourteen-item questionnaire distributed to European American undergraduate students at Arctica University and African American graduate students at Antarctica University. The initial study utilized a qualitative method, while the secondary study utilized a quantitative method. Most of the respondents were recruited in person from their respective campuses. The two students who were not approached in person for the focus groups were recruited via flyers posted in the residence halls and cafeterias. Upon initial contact, I explained the nature and significance of the study and encouraged voluntary participation for a one-hour focus group. In the case of the survey study, the multicultural affairs office at Antarctica University assisted in the distribution of the questionnaires. Several instructors at Arctica University allowed students time to complete the surveys during the first few minutes of their classes.

The initial study required focus groups composed of from six to eight individuals over the age of seventeen with the equivalent of at least one year's college education. The age range of the African American focus group was eighteen to thirty-eight; the age range for the European American focus group was twenty-six to forty-five. The African American (AA) respondents were classified as follows: two were sophomores, three were juniors, and one was a senior. Among the European American (EA) respondents were four medical students and two occupational therapy students. The average years of educational experience was three for both groups. All of the students were students at schools located in the District of Columbia. The secondary study involved thirty students, fifteen recruited from each university. The age range of the survey respondents was deemed impertinent for the secondary study. Among the African American graduate respondents were six law students, four engineering students, two accounting students, one chemistry student, one education student, and one social work student. The European American undergraduate students were classified as follows: ten pre-pharmacy students, two biology students, two English students, and one pre-medical student. The average years of experience was three for the undergraduate students, and two-and-a-half for the graduate students.

Each of the focus group subjects was invited to a one-hour interview. There were six interviewees in each focus group. A consent form approved by the Institutional Review Boards at both Howard and American universities was used to gain the consent of the participants to audiotape the discussion. The discussions took place in classrooms at the respective universities.

After data was collected from each group, the researcher transcribed the data, a task that took forty-five hours to complete. Subsequently, Glaser and Strauss's constant comparison method was utilized to analyze and interpret the data.

A secondary study was implemented to verify the results acquired from the initial study. Furthermore, the second study sought to correct the disparity between the perspectives of graduate and undergraduate students. One female

European American focus group interviewee claimed that age and educational experience exempted her from being concerned about cultural identity negotiation. As a result, the first item of the distributed survey asked whether the respondent agreed with the following statement: "Graduate students negotiate cultural identity just as much as undergraduate students." (An explanation of cultural negotiation of cultural identity is given on the survey.) The questionnaire was designed not only to answer the research questions, but also to discover whether years of educational experience had any effect on perceptions of identity maturity. The consistencies and disparities of the survey responses was identified in order to determine whether the secondary study positively verified the initial focus group investigation.

SUMMARY OF THE RESEARCH QUESTIONS

The accomplishment of each of the aforementioned objectives is outlined within this chapter. The following headings directly correspond with the research questions presented in Chapter 6.

Relational Aspects

By collecting data from two different focus groups, the researcher was better able to account for the relationship between African Americans and European Americans. Each perspective was distinct. The two sets of respondents reported different dimensions of the ongoing discourse between the two cultures. While European Americans indicated a preference for racial homogeneity, African Americans resisted harmony with European Americans. African American students further expressed an emphatic rejection of "color-blindness."

Causes of Cultural Identity Negotiation

The advantages of a qualitative approach were most evident while gathering data regarding the causes of cultural identity negotiation. The African American respondents, who immediately understood what cultural identity negotiation was, offered extensive rationale for negotiating cultural identity. These are presented in chapter 4 under theme 10. Their responses indicated the belief that African Americans are most willing to exchange or reconsider at least part of their cultural identities if they lack self-esteem, think they can get ahead in some way, seek White persons' approval, maintain a "White mentality," or were "nurtured that way to be around these people."

Need for Cultural Self-Definition (RQ #1)

It was discovered as a result of the focus group interviews that European American students believed their culture was American. When asked to define American culture, three of the male interviewees reported, "You can't really call it anything in particular, it's whatever you want it to be. American culture is so hard, you can't really define it. I mean it is, that's it." One of the female interviewees responded, "I never really thought about it. I know I'm European Irish, but I know that's not really who I am."

African American interviewees expressed a different need. Each of the respondents indicated the necessity of having a solid cultural identity. Three of the female interviewees suggested, "I think you have to have a cultural identity in general just so you know who you are and where you come from. You really do because people will, not attack you, but challenge who you are, and you really have to accept who you are as a person in society/ We can't shed this Blackness, as soon as you walk out there in the world, you're already judged. What you can do, what you can't do, where you came from, how you talk, how you dress, what your parents do, how intelligent you are, what you're capable of doing in the future." Moreover, the one male respondent claimed that these things force African Americans to develop a cultural self-awareness.

The secondary study verified the findings of the focus group investigation. It was discovered after conducting two t tests that European American students at Arctica university and African American students at Antarctica university significantly differed ($t = 3.64$, $p < .01$) in the way that they defined themselves culturally. Xavier students suggested a tendency to equate their culture with American culture, while Tulane students suggested that their culture was completely distinctive from American culture. Furthermore, when asked if they defined themselves on the basis of their ancestral heritage, European Americans suggested otherwise. The two sets of respondents differed significantly ($t=6.32$, $p < .01$) in their responses. The African American students indicated strong agreement with needing to define themselves on the basis of their ancestral heritage.

Process of Cultural Identity Negotiation (RQ#2)

Neither set of respondents claimed to negotiate identity. The researcher solicited reasons for not negotiating. Justifications differed. The European American subjects never negotiated. One male respondent exclaimed, "Negotiating cultural identity is kind of a vague term and I don't really think it applies in any situation." Another male interviewee admitted, "We are the dominant culture. . . and I think in order to make it in this world, in order to be prosperous, in order to raise a family, I think you have to be a part of that dominant, and I think for African Americans, they have to make changes."

One African American female respondent claimed, "I cannot negotiate my person . . . . Black people have negotiated too much over the years and that's exactly what the problem is. We're too passive." Another female subject remarked, "I think we have come far enough now, we don't need to do that. Before it was called uncle-tomming and it was done for a purpose then, but we don't need to tom anymore." While neither set of respondents claimed to engage in a process of cultural identity negotiation, an African American female respondent hypothesized that identity negotiation begins "the minute they question who they are and are embarrassed by who they are."

The survey study confirmed the results of the focus groups by finding no significant differences in the responses of the two sets of subjects ($z = 1.00$, $p < .01$).

Consequences, Motivation, Conditions, and Duration (RQ's #3 and 4)

Again, neither group admitted to negotiating cultural identity. Even after extensively elaborating on the concept, the European American respondents indicated their inability to understand why they would need to do so; one male respondent asked the researcher how he could change, alter, or reconsider his cultural identity. Because the European American subjects did not see the importance of negotiating their cultural identities, neither could they fathom any consequences. A female respondent finally lamented that she did not have time to worry about cultural identity and its negotiation. She equated this type of concern with an undergraduate search for social approval.

The African American students suggested that they could not live with themselves if they had to forfeit their integrity by negotiating who they are. Further comments depicted a concern for the progress of the African American culture. A female respondent intuited, "We need to stop acting like we are the world and stop compromising our values. It takes us back, and we'll never go forward in believing in ourselves as a people."

The motivations are clearly articulated under theme 10 in chapter 4. The conditions under which one is most likely to reconsider or replace cultural identity are also subsumed under theme 10. Generally, each set of interviewees indicated that there are no conditions under which they would reconsider their own cultural identities. The African American students predicted that others would possibly reconsider or replace their cultural identities due to some sort of expected advancement, maintenance of another culture's worldview, or a poor self esteem.

The duration of the negotiation process was not discussed, except in the statements indicating that African Americans must come to the institution with a cultural identity or willingness to develop an African American identity. Otherwise, the consequences were to be what was described as "lost."

DISCUSSION AND IMPLICATIONS

Summary of Findings, Interpretation, and Literature Support

This investigation empirically considered three assumptions that are widely held by African Americans; first, European Americans do not find it necessary to define themselves culturally; second, they do not need to significantly alter their behavior though they study at an African American university; finally, there are virtually no conscious, long-term identity consequences associated with the adjustment possibly made by European Americans at an African American university.

The experiment with methods required hand-selecting of respondents, audiotaping, transcribing, and coding themes for the focus group interviewees. Moreover, the triangulated method involved the combination of an interpretive and a functionalist approach to the investigation's research questions.

Several findings of this investigation are significant. First, the European American respondents endorsed a homogeneous classification of all citizens and residents of the United States as "American." African Americans claim African American culture and a need to distinctively define themselves culturally. The survey responses revealed that almost all (n = 11) of the African American respondents indicated that their culture was distinct from American culture. Furthermore, they believed that their culture needed to be defined on the basis of their ancestral heritage. Secondly, because European Americans described their culture and that of African Americans as "basically the same," the process of negotiation was deemed counterproductive. African Americans felt just the opposite. They described their culture as being distinctive and communicated the need to maintain its distinguishing properties. Additionally, it seemed that the older students in both focus groups believed that cultural identity negotiation was a social adjustment reserved for undergraduate students, although, the oldest African American student still expressed a need for cultural self-definition. The basic finding was that the negotiation of cultural identity was experienced neither by the African American nor European American students. Yet, the reasons for not negotiating differed for each. The reasons reported by European Americans were homogeneity, graduate/professional student status, and lack of time. Those reported by African Americans were homogeneity (color-blindness), cultural dignity, personal integrity, pride, and that "we cannot afford to."

Cultural identity negotiation is potentially a subconscious phenomenon for the European American students. On the other hand, the African American students are quite conscious of cultural identity negotiation. It could be that the African American focus group participants are subconsciously engaged in negotiation; however, the present study only considers information reported above or at levels of consciousness, but not below.

Recent research supports the idea that African Americans are at least concerned about cultural negotiation of identity (Hare, 1991; Wilson, 1990). Additionally, conditions effecting negotiation are well-cited (Ani, 1994, Baldwin, 1991; Fanon, 1967; Millionnes, 1980).

The conclusion of the study is that the conscious negotiation of cultural identity is not experienced by either group of individuals. However, it has historically been a marginalized group phenomenon, and the respondents gave testimony of this. European American respondents were not concerned about cultural identity negotiation because it had never been experienced by them personally, nor did they have any knowledge of it being experienced by other members of their culture. Negotiation of cultural identity, while not presently experienced by the African American interviewees, is nonetheless a concern of theirs. Their active resistance to it testifies to their concern; thus this empirical study concludes that it is a marginalized group phenomenon. This is partially determined as well by the intensity with which African American respondents reported their feelings and opinions about the avoidance of identity negotiation.

The analysis of the data collected relative to the principle objectives of the study suggests that the first four steps of the Third Culture Building model are relatively automatic, and may transpire rather quickly. The fifth stage, however, is crucial. This stage, "mutual adjustment," requires that one question his or her values, beliefs, and mores, eliminate some cultural constructions, and replace them with a mutually decided-upon substitute. Culturally, the data proves that third culture building is not only risky, but is often avoided, unless necessary. African American respondents clearly resist exchange of cultural components.

European American respondents seem willing but unclear about what to relinquish. The first step in any negotiation is knowing what is being exchanged. The European American students found difficulty in defining what it meant to be American, yet that was the culture they claimed. Negotiation would be virtually impossible without a clear understanding of what it is that is being negotiated.

Hecht, Collier, and Ribeau's communication theory of ethnic identity is also applicable. The sensitizing constructs considered within this investigation were core symbols, codes, prescriptions, and community. First, "core symbols" are defined as expressions of cultural beliefs and understandings. The core symbols expressed by European American students from Pacifica university (PU) to describe their culture were the following: a picnic on Memorial Day; fireworks on the Fourth of July; *Gilligan's Island* and *Brady Bunch* reruns; power; and military dominance. The African American students at Atlantica university (AU) identified struggle, power, progress, beauty, music, matriarchal family structure, and spirituality as core symbols.

Second, each group of participants noted certain perceptions about codes held by the "other culture." "Codes" are defined as a set of symbols and meanings based on a worldview. While neither group spoke extensively of the "other's" codes, the PU students believed them to be "the handshake," dancing, and slang for African Americans. The AU students mentioned flags as being a code for Italian cultural pride. It appeared as though Italians were grouped by these students within the category of "White culture" (see Theme 13).

Third, "prescriptions" are the rules guiding behavior and appropriate conduct. Each set of students commented on their own prescriptions and those of the other culture. Students at PU expressed a concern for intermingling. Being at an "all-white" table or suddenly realizing that several "Whites" are walking in a group to Taco Bell are sensitive topics. The guiding rule according to an European American male medical student is that "you interact enough to get comfortable, but not to fit in." One PU student clearly indicated his belief that African Americans must change who they are, so that at least their behaviors more closely resemble that of European Americans.

Atlantica university students seemed to suggest that a prescribed rule for African American cultural survival is not to negotiate cultural identity. Specific to the experiences on a predominantly European American campus, it was asserted several times within the one-hour interview that African American students come to school with their cultural identities already intact. Their perception of European Americans is that they maintain a code of expectation; in other words, they expect African Americans to change who they are or how they behave in order to resemble more closely the behaviors of European Americans.

Finally, each group expresses their own notions of community, or cultural cohesiveness. The European American students at Pacifica university indicated that American culture is whatever one wants it to be. It is virtually undefinable, because of its unending possibilities. Community is expressed by the shared perception among the respondents that everyone in America is basically the same, with minor differences. There was a common concern for academic goal-achievement and some sense of power as members of the dominant culture.

African American students at AU find their cohesiveness in the common struggle experienced by all African Americans. There was a general consensus among the participants that the term "Black" was all-encompassing. Consequently, it was a preferred term, since it included all Black people, whether they are born in Brazil, the Caribbean, an African country, or anywhere else.

Both focus group interviews examined identity as a communicated process of self-development. The European American students described various conflicts, surprises, and other occurrences which had transpired via interaction with African Americans at PU. The African American students at AU explained their concerns and strategies of securing cultural identity which emerged as a result of having interacted with European Americans at AU.

The survey data from the secondary study gave a positive verification of the results from the focus group interviews. The same results were achieved outside of the vicinity of Washington D.C., and were discovered using a quantitative approach. The African American focus group interviewees at Atlantica university suggested that the cultural identity negotiation process is initiated when one begins to question his or her own values and beliefs. Seventy-three percent (n = 11) of both sample populations reported a strong disagreement to having felt pressure to question their cultural identities. This lack of questioning cultural self-definition verifies one of the findings from the focus group study, which revealed that the process is stagnated by the unwillingness to negotiate or reconsider their cultural identities. Starosta and Olorunnisola's (Chen and Starosta, 1998) Third Culture Building model is also prevented from moving forward at this point. Furthermore, these survey questions verified additional focus group results, which are as follows: European American students do not feel the need to behaviorally or communicatively codeswitch; European Americans are not pressured to redefine their cultural identities; and European Americans are less likely to negotiate.

Discussion of Problems and Limitations

Four problems encountered in the process of implementing this research study which should be considered when examining the limitations of the data.

First, the investigation was able to gather only ideas above the level of consciousness. While this may not seem to be a remediable concern, it is still a limitation, since most respondents are unable to articulate what their identities mean to them, because they have not thought very much about it. The study may have yielded different results otherwise. The only remedy to this problem is to practice facilitation skills, prepare the group to open up (maybe with an exercise), and ask the respondent to be as specific as possible. Yet, the researcher still runs the risk of having a set of low self-monitors.

Second, it is always a threat to the consistency of ideas when the interviewer is not an ingroup member of the respondents'culture. Perhaps the comments would have been different had I been a White person talking to the White focus group interviewees.

Another problem was the time spent transcribing. I would recommend applying for a grant or some other funding to have this done at no expense to the researcher. This process was very time-consuming. If an expense must be incurred, it should be an anticipated cost in the project budget.

Finally, in the initial study the European American students were all graduate students in the health sciences. As I began to examine the parent population of European American students at Arctica university, another HBCU, it was clear that many of the European American students were attending HBCU's to major in the health sciences. Moreover, students enrolling in these HBCU's are often graduate, professional, pre-professional, or transfer students. Consequently, this limitation is unavoidable unless data is gathered from an HBCU that has a large European American population. This would, of course, pose a greater threat to the study, since the likelihood of cultural identity negotiation would probably decrease as the parent population increases.

Discussion of the Practical Implications

A number of findings derived from the study may have practical implications for others involved in research or applied practice in a related area such as management, social work, psychology, communication, or education.

Middle or upper-level managers within private or public industry organizations may find that employees have low morale, low productivity, or damaging coworker relationships. This study may assist organizational leaders in diagnosing the problem. It could be that a culturally diverse set of employees is tired of negotiating their identities on the job or elsewhere. This constant codeswitching produces both employee resistance and fatigue .

Counselors may also find this research valuable. Often, therapists administer large doses of sedatives, tranquilizers, or other drugs to calm a patient. It could be that the patient is empowering him/herself to behave this way due to feelings of exclusion or isolation. As the present investigation indicates, self-empowerment is one of the reactions of an identity in the process of negotiation. Academic advisors may be benefited as well by exercising greater sensitivity toward international students, especially after reviewing the discussion of race, ethnicity, and culture in Chapter 2.

Of course, identity specialists would find this research helpful, since it explores an unpaved ground within Communication. Also, it systematically examines cultural identity as both a negotiation process and definition. Communication scholars may find that cultural identity negotiation is a valuable way to consider rhetorical, intrapersonal, interpersonal, intercultural, and international relationships.

Education is an especially useful forum for observing cultural identity negotiation at work. Recently, many primary and secondary institutions have taken extensive measures to secure their buildings with metal detectors, armed guards, and "gun-collection Fridays." The students are attempting to assert who they are and what they represent; if no one listens or seeks to understand them, criminally delinquent expressions of hidden hostility will continue. The students, like most young adults, want to be heard. If their voice is excluded, consequences can be deleterious. Utilizing the framework, design, and analytical technique, identity research may be applied in these varied arenas.

SUGGESTIONS FOR FUTURE RESEARCH

Emanating from this study came several different directions for future research. Only four are presented here. First, I recommend using the same design to explore the attitude and behavioral implications of Black conservatives in comparison to Black radicals. Of particular use to this exploration might be the revised nigrescence model presented by Cross and Fhagen-Smith (1995). As noted earlier, these authors consider the "ideological splits" of persons who score high with regards to their levels of ego-development and internalization.

Secondly, a rhetorical analysis of Black militant leaders turned conservative would be an interesting direction for future research, using Starosta's (1974) adaptation of Kenneth Burke's cluster analysis.

Thirdly, a systematic examination of intracultural negotiation among African Americans would be an heuristic contribution to the study of cultural identity as a communicated phenomenon. The design used within the present study would yield rich data explaining this process. Or, this framework might be applied to examining the attitudes and opinions of African Americans within the African American community at large.

Fourthly, a different methodological approach might be explored, such as a regression analysis combined with extended interviews. This would preserve the triangulated method and still provide a unique heuristic contribution.

Finally, the most natural direction for this research is to ground a theory of cultural identity negotiation, since Glaser and Strauss's (1967) constant comparison technique is a grounded theory model anyway. A different culture might be examined and compared; maybe Asian American students could be compared to African American students in terms of adjustment and codeswitching behaviors.

The entire discussion of race, ethnicity, and culture in America is considered to be a very disruptive and yet it is still a necessary engagement. As Cornel West points out in *Race Matters*, the concept of race seems to be a parasitic insect that consumes the US. Nowhere else in the world, he claims, is this so ingrained in the minds, hearts, and sensibilities of the general populace. It is amazing that something so minor as skin color, a phylocentric constant in the human equation, can disrupt relationships, ruin aspirations and possibilities, and most importantly, prevent social cohesion. But it has, and it does. It will continue to do so unless scholars become activists ordinary citizens become social change agents, and the United States of America learns to humble herself enough to be self-critical. Until this happens, the negotiation of cultural identity will be a prevalent germ of frustration and discontent. It will be the inescapable social legacy and political stain of marginalized groups, perpetually transmitted to successive generations. The discussion of race and culture is a necessary engagement, because the concept of race is a manufactured thread within the fabric of the American ethos. We cannot and must not seek to escape or circumvent it; rather we must confront it directly, restore equitable social, political and economic opportunity to all communities, and then eliminate race as a social microbe and inhibitive mechanism within the United States of America. Our challenge as a nation has never been greater !

Bibliography

Abrahams, R. (1970). *Positively Black*. Englewood Cliffs, NJ: Prentice-Hall.

Akbar, N. (1991). The evolution of human psychology for African Americans. In R.L. Jones (ed.), *Black Psychology*. Berkeley, CA: Cobb and Henry.

Allport, G. (1954). *The nature of prejudice*. Reading, Massachusetts: Addison-Wesley Publishing Company.

Amir, Y. (1969). Contact hypothesis in ethnic relations. *Psychological Bulletin,* 71: 319-331.

Ani, M. (1994). *Yurugu*. Trenton, N.J.: Africa World Press.

Asante, M. K. (1978). Intercultural communication: An Afrocentric inquiry into encounter. In Bruce Williams and Orlando Taylor (eds.) *International Conference on Black Communication: A Bellagio Conference*. NY: Rockefeller Foundation.

------------ (1980). *Afrocentricity*. Trenton, N.J.: Africa World Press.

------------ (1987). *The Afrocentric Idea*. Philadelphia: Temple University Press.

------------ (1990). *Kemet, Africentricity, and Knowledge*. Trenton, N.J.: Africa World Press.

------------ (1993). *Malcolm X as Cultural Hero and Other Afrocentric Essays*. Trenton, N.J.: Africa World Press.

Baldwin, J. (1963). *The Fire Next Time*. NY: The Dial Press.

Baldwin, J. A. (1980). The psychology of oppression. In M.K. Asante and A. Vandi (eds.), *Contemporary Black Thought*. Beverly Hills, CA: Sage.

------------ (1991). *African (Black) Psychology: Issues and Synthesis*. (pp. 125-140). Berkeley, CA: Cobb and Henry.

Baldwin, J. A., R. Brown, and R. Hopkins (1991). The Black self-hatred paradigm revisited: Africentric analysis. In R.L. Jones (ed.), *Black Psychology*. (pp. 141-166). Berkeley, CA: Cobb and Henry.

Bandura, A. (1971). *Social Learning Theory*. Morristown, NJ: General Learning Press.

Banks, J.A. (1981). Stages of ethnicity: Implications for curriculum reform. In J.A. Banks (ed.), *Multiethnic Education: Theory and Practice*. (pp.129-139). Boston: Allyn and Bacon.

Banton, M. (1983). *Racial and Ethnic Competition*. Cambridge: Cambridge University Press.

Barbu, Z. (1971). *Society, Culture, and Personality.* NY: Schocken Books.

Bell, D. (1975). Ethnicity and social change. In N. Glazer and D. Moynihan (eds.), *Ethnicity: Theory and Experience.* Cambridge, MA: Harvard Press.

Berger, C. R. and J. Bradac (1982). *Language and Social Knowledge: Uncertainty in Interpersonal Relations.* London: Edward Arnold.

Berger, C. R. and R. J. Calabrese (1975). Some explorations in initial interaction and beyond. *Human Communication Research,* 1: 99-112.

Berger, P. and Luckmann, T. (1967). *The Social Construction of Reality.* NY, NY: Penguin.

Berne, E. (1964). *Games People Play: The Psychology of Human Relationships.* NY: Grove.

Bernstein, B. (1966). Elaborated and restricted codes: their social origins and some consequences. In J. Gumperz and Dell Hymes (eds.), *American Anthropologist,* 66(6): 2.

Binet, A. and T. Simon (1911). *A Method of Measuring the Development of the Intelligence of Young Children.* Lincoln, IL.: Courier.

Blau, P. M. (1964). *Exchange and power in social life.* NY: Wiley.

Blumenbach, J. F. (1825). *A Manual of the Elements of Natural History.* London: Simpkin and Marshall.

Boynton, J. A. (1941). Racial stereotypes of Negro college students. *Journal of Abnormal and Social Psychology,* 36: 97-102.

Bracey, J., A. Meier and E. Rudwick (1973). The Black sociologists: The first half century. In J. A. Ladner (ed.), *The Death of White Sociology.* (pp. 3-18) NY: Random House.

Brewer, M. B. and D. T. Campbell (1976). *Ethnocentrism and Intergroup Attitudes.* NY: Halstead.

Burke, P. J. and J. Tully (1977). The measurement of role/identity. *Social Forces,* 55: 881-897.

Burkitt, I. (1992). *Social selves: theories of the social formation of personality.* London: Sage.

Burlew, A. K. and L. Smith (1991). Measures of racial identity: An overview of a proposed framework. *The Journal of Black Psychology,* 17(2): 53-71.

Carmichael, S. (K. Ture) and C. Hamilton (1967/1992). *Black power: The politics of liberation.* NY: Vintage.

Carruthers, J. (1972). *Science and oppression.* Chicago: Center for inner city studies, Northeastern Illinois University.

Carter, R. T. and J. E. Helms (1987). The relationship of Black value-orientations to racial identity attitudes. *Measurement and Evaluation in Counseling and Development,* 19: 185-195.

Cassell, J. (1977). The relationship of observer in peer group research. *Human Organization,* 36(4): 412-416.

Chen, G. M. and W. J. Starosta (1998). *Foundations of Intercultural Communication.* Needham Heights, MA: Allyn & Bacon.

Clark, K. and M. Clark (1947). Racial identification and preferences in Negro children. *Readings in Social Psychology.* NY: Holt.

Collier, M. J. and M. Thomas (1988). Cultural identity: an interpretive perspective. In Y.Y. Kim and W.B. Gudykunst (eds.), *Theories in Intercultural Communication* (pp. 99-120). Newbury Park, CA: Sage.

Collier, M. J. and M. Thomas (1989). Cultural identity in inter-cultural communication: An interpretive perspective. In W.B. Gudykunst and Y.Y. Kim (eds.), *Theorizing Intercultural Communication: International and Intercultural Communication Annual, 12* (pp. 94-120). Newbury Park, CA: Sage.

Collins, P. H. (1990). The social construction of Black feminist thought. In M. Malson, E. Mudumbe-Boyi, J. O'Barr, and M. Wyer (eds.), *Black Women in*

America (pp. 297-326). Chicago: University of Chicago Press.

Conrad, E. (1966). *The Invention of the Negro.* NY: Paul Eriksson.

Cross, W. E. (1971). The Negro to Black conversion experience: Towards the psychology of Black liberation. *Black World,* 20: 13-27.

Cross, W.E. and P. Fhagen-Smith (1995). Nigrescence and ego identity development: Accounting for differential Black identity patterns. In P. Pedersen, J. Draguns, W. Lonner, and J. Trimble (eds.), *Counseling Across Cultures.* (pp. 108-123). Thousand Oaks, CA: Sage.

Cupach, W.R. and B. H. Spitzberg (1983). Trait versus state: A comparison of dispositional and situational measures of interpersonal communication competence. *Western Journal of Speech Communication,* 47: 364-379.

Darwin, C. (1859). *The Origin of Species.* London: Penguin Books.

Davis, A. (1983). *Women, Race, and Class.* NY: Vintage Press.

Davis, T.E. (1937). Some racial attitudes of Negro college and grade school students. *Journal of Negro Education,* 6: 157-165.

DeCoy, R.H. (1987). *The Nigger Bible.* Los Angeles: Holloway House Publishing.

Delia, J. and R. Clark (1977). Cognitive complexity, social perception and the development of listener-adapted communication in six-, eight-, ten-, and twelve-year-old boys. *Communication Monographs,* 44(4): 326-345.

Devereux, G. (1975). Ethnic identity: Its logical foundations and dysfunctions. In G. De Vos and L. Romanucci-Ross (eds.). *Ethnic Identity: Cultural Continuities and Change* (p. 43). Palo Alto, CA: Mayfield Press.

De Tocqueville, A. (1832/1956). *Democracy in America.* NY: Vintage Books.

De Vos, G.A. (1982). Ethnic pluralism: Conflict and accommodation. In G.A. De Vos and L. Romanucci-Ross (eds.), *Ethnic Identity: Cultural Continuities and change* (pp. 5-41). Chicago: University of Chicago Press.

Diamond, S. and B. Belasco (1980). Biological and cultural evolution. In I. Rossi (ed.) *People in Culture: A Survey of Cultural Anthropology.* NY: Praeger.

Dickens, F. and Dickens, J. (1992). *The Black Manager: Making It in the Corporate World.* NY: Amacom.

Diop, C.A. (1991). *Civilization or Barbarism: An Authentic Anthropology.* Chicago: Lawrence Hill.

Dixon, V. J. (1976). World views and research methodology. In L. King et al. (eds.), *African Philosophy: Assumptions and Paradigms for Research on Black Persons.* Los Angeles: Fanon Center.

Du Bois, W. E. B. (1899). The Philadelphia Negro. *Outlook,* 63: 647-648.

------------ (1903). *The Souls of Black Folk.* Chicago: A.C. McClurg.

------------ (1915). *The Negro.* NY: Henry Holt.

Dyal, J. and R. Dyal (1981). Acculturation, stress, and coping. *International Journal of Intercultural Relations,* 5: 301-328.

Ellison, R. (1973). An American dilemma: A review. In J.A. Ladner (ed.), *The Death of White Sociology.* (pp. 81-95). NY: Random House.

Fager, C. (1967). *White Reflections on Black Power.* Grand rapids, MI: Eerdman's.

Fanon, F. (1963). *The Wretched of the Earth.* NY: Grove Press.

------------ (1967). *Black Skin White Masks.* NY: Grove Press.

Farr, R. (1990). Waxing and waning of interest in Societal Psychology: A historical perspective. In H. T. Himmelweit and G. Gaskell (eds.), *Societal Psychology.* London: Sage.

Fellows, D. K. (1972). *A Mosaic of America's Ethnic Minorities.* NY: John Wiley and Sons.

Fine, M. A., A. I. Schwebel and L. J. Myers (1985). The effects of world view adaptation to single parenthood among middle-class adult women. *Journal of Family Issues,* 6: 107-127.

Frazier, E. Franklin (1963). *The Negro Church in America.* London: University of Liverpool.

Freire, P. (1983). *Pedagogy of the Oppressed.* NY: Continuum.

Frideres, J. and S. Goldenberg (1982). Ethnic identity: Myth and reality in Western Canada. *International Journal of Intercultural Relations,* 6: 137-151.

Gallois, C., A. Franklyn-Stokes, H. Giles and N. Coupland (1988). Communication accommodation in intercultural encounters. In Y.Y. Kim and W.B. Gudykunst (eds.), *Theories in Intercultural Communication* (pp. 157-185). Newbury Park, CA: Sage.

Geertz, C. (1973). *The Interpretation of Cultures.* NY: Basic Books.

Gergen, K.J. (1994). *Toward Transformation in Social knowledge.* NY: Springer-Verlag.

Gibran, K. (1926/1991). *Sand and Foam.* NY: Alfred Knopf Publishers.

Giles, H., R. Y. Bourhis, and D. Taylor (1977). Towards a theory of language in ethnic group relations. In H. Giles and R. St. Clair (eds.), *Language, Ethnicity, and Intergroup Relations* (pp.307-348). London: Academic Press.

Giles, H. and P. Johnson (1981). The role of language in ethnic group relations. In J. Turner and H. Giles (eds.), *Intergroup Behavior* (pp. 199-242). Chicago: University of Chicago Press.

Giles, H., N. Coupland and J. Coupland (1991). Accommodation theory: Communication, contexts, and consequences. In H. Giles, N. Coupland, and J. Coupland (eds.), *Contexts of Accommodation: Developments in Applied Sociolinguistics* (pp. 1-68). Cambridge: Cambridge University Press.

Glaser, B. and A. Strauss (1967). *The Discovery of Grounded Theory: Strategies for Qualitative Research.* Chicago: Aldine.

Glazer, N. and D. Moynihan (1975). Introduction. In N. Glazer and D. Moynihan (eds.), *Ethnicity: Theory and Experience.* London: Harvard University Press.

Gobineau, A. (1853/1967). *The Inequality of Human Races.* NY: Howard Fertig.

Goddard, H. H. (1914). *Feeble-mindedness: Its Causes and Consequences.* NY: MacMillan.

------------ (1919). *Psychology of the Normal and Subnormal.* NY: Dodd, Mead, and Company.

Goffman, E. (1959). *The presentation of Self in Everyday Life.* Garden City, NY: Doubleday Press.

------------ (1961). *Asylums.* NY: Doubleday.

Gossett, T. (1965). *Race: The History of an Idea in America.* NY: Schocken.

Gould, S. (1981). *The Mismeasure of Man.* NY: Norton.

Gramsci, A. (1983). *Selections from Prison Notebooks.* NY: International.

Grier, W. H. and P. M. Cobbs (1968). *Black rage.* NY: Basic Books.

Guba, E. and Y. Lincoln (1981). *Effective Evaluation.* San Francisco, CA: Jossey-Bass.

Gudykunst, W. B. and M. Hammer (1988). The influence on social identity and intimacy of interethnic relationships on uncertainty reduction processes. *Human Communication Research,* 14: 569-601.

Gudykunst, W. B. and T. Lim (1986). A perspective for the study of intergroup communication. In W.B. Gudykunst (ed.), *Intergroup Communication.* (pp. 1-9). Baltimore, MD: Edward Arnold.

Gudykunst, W. B. and T. Nishida (1984). Individual and cultural influences on uncertainty reduction. *Communication Monographs,* 51: 23-26.

Gudykunst, W.B. and T. Nishida (1989). Theoretical perspectives for studying intercultural communication. In M. K. Asante and W. B. Gudykunst (eds.), *Handbook of International and Intercultural Communication.* Newbury Park, CA: Sage.

Guthrie, R. (1976). *Even the Rat Was White.* NY: Harper and Row.

Hacker, A. (1992). *Two Nations: Black and White, Separate, Hostile, unequal.* NY: MacMillan Publishing Co.

Hall, E. T. (1959). *The Silent Language.* Garden City, NY: Anchor.

Hammer, M. (1989). Intercultural communication competence. In M.K. Asante and W.B. Gudykunst (eds.), *Handbook of International and Intercultural Communication.* (pp. 247-260). London: Sage.

Harding, J., B. Kutner, H. Prohansky, and I. Chein (1954). Prejudice and ethnic relations. In G. Lindsey (ed.), *Handbook of Social Psychology, 2.* Reading, MA: Addison-Wesley.

Hare, N. (1991). *The Black Anglo-Saxons.* Chicago: Third World Press.

Harre, R. (1979). Language games and texts of identity. In J. Shotter and K.J. Gergen (eds.), *Texts of Identity* (pp. 20-35). Newbury Park, CA: Sage.

Harre, R. and P. Secord (1972). *The Explanation of Social Behavior.* Oxford: Basil Blackwell.

Haskins, J. and H. Butts (1973). *Psychology of Black Language.* NY: Hippocrene.

Hecht, M. (1993). 2002-Research odyssey: Toward the development of a communication theory of identity. *Communication Monographs,* 60: 77-82.

Hecht, M., M. J. Collier, and S. Ribeau (1993). *African American Communication: Ethnic Identity and Cultural Interpretation.* Newbury Park, CA: Sage.

Hecht, M. and S. Ribeau (1984). Ethnic communication: A comparative analysis of satisfying communication. *International Journal of Intercultural Relations,* 8: 135-151.

Hecht, M., S. Ribeau and J. Alberts (1989). An Afro-American perspective on interethnic communication. *Communication Monographs,* 56: 384-410.

Hegel, G.W.F. (1899/1956). *The Philosophy of History.* NY: Holt.

Helms, J.E. (1990). An overview of Black racial identity theory. In J.E. Helms (ed.), *Black and White racial identity: Theory, Research, and Practice* (pp. 9-32). Westport, CT: Greenwood Press.

Herskovits, M. (1941). *The myth of the Negro past.* Boston: Beacon Press.

Hewitt, J. P. (1988). *Self and Society.* Boston: Allyn and Bacon.

Hewstone, M. and R. Brown (1986). Contact is not enough: An intergroup perspective on the "contact hypothesis." In M. Hewstone and R. Brown (eds.), *Contact and Conflict in Intergroup Encounters* (pp. 1-44). London: Basil Blackwell.

Hewstone, M. and J. Jaspers (1982). Intergroup relations and attributional processes. In H. Tajfel (ed.), *Social Identity and Intergroup Relations.* Cambridge: Cambridge University Press.

Hirsch, C. (1972). *The Riddle of Racism.* NY: Viking Press.

Hofstede, G. (1980). *Culture Consequences.* Beverly Hills, CA: Sage.

Holloway, J. E. (1990). Introduction. In J.E. Holloway (ed.), *Africanisms.* Bloomington, IN: Indiana University Press.

Holzner, B. and R. Robertson (1979). Identity and authority: A problem analysis of the processes of identification and authorization. In R.Robertson and B. Holzner (eds.), *Identity and Authority.* NY: St. Martin's Press.

Homans, G. C. (1974). *Social Behavior: Its Elementary Forms.* NY:

Harcourt, Brace, and Jovanovich.
     Horney, K. (1950). *Neurosis and Human Growth: The Struggle Toward Self-realization.* NY: W.W. Norton.
     Horton, P. and C. Hunt (1964). *Sociology.* (2nd ed.). NY: McGraw Hill.
     Horwitz, D. (1975). Ethnic identity. In N. Glazer and D. Moynihan (eds.), *Ethnicity: Theory and Experience* (pp. 111-140). Cambridge, MA: Harvard University Press.
     Hraba, J. (1979). *American Ethnicity.* (p.27) Itasca, IL: Peacock Publishers.
     Ibrahim, F. A. and H. Kahn (1987). Assessment of world views. *Psychological Reports,* 60: 163-176.
     Infante, D., D. Womack and A. Rancer (1990). *Building Communication Theory.* Prospect Heights, IL.: Waveland Press.
     Jackson, B. (1976). Black identity development. In L. Gloubshick and B. Persky (eds.), *Urban Social and Educational Issues.* (pp. 158-164). Dubuque: Kendall-Hall.
     Jackson, R.L. (February 1999). White Space, White Privilege: Mapping discursive inquiry into the self. *Quarterly Journal of Speech, 55(1),* 1-17.
     Janis, I. (1982). *Groupthink.* (2nd ed.). Boston: Houghton-Mifflin.
     Jones, J. (1991). The concept of race in social psychology. In R.L. Jones (ed.), *Black Psychology.* (pp. 441-468). Berkeley, CA: Cobb and Henry.
     Jones, R. (1985). *Research Methods in the Social and Behavioral Sciences.* (pp. 142-168). Sunderland, MA: Sinauer Associates.
     Jordan, W. (1968). *White over Black: American Attitudes Toward the Negro, 1550-1812.* Chapel Hill, NC: University of North Carolina Press.
     Jung, K. (1961). *Symbols and Transformation.* Princeton, N.J.: Princeton University Press.
     Kardiner, A. and L. Ovessey (1951). *The Mark of Oppression.* NY: Norton.
     Keane-Dawes, J. (1995). *A Critical-interpretive Approach to Stigma: Variations in Responses of Culturally Diverse Jamaican and American deaf groups.* Lanham, MD: University Press of America
     Kelves, D. J. (1985). *In the Name of Eugenics: Genetics and the Uses of Human Heredity.* NY: Knopf.
     Kerlinger, F. (1986). *Foundations of Behavioral Research.* NY: Holt, Rinehart, and Winston.
     Kim, M. and W. Sharkey (1995). Independent and interdependent construals of self: Explaining cultural patterns of interpersonal communication in multi-cultural organizational settings. *Communication Quarterly, 43(1),* 20-38.
     Kim, Y. Y. (1986). Introduction: A communication approach to interethnic relations. In Y. Y. Kim (ed.), *Interethnic Communication: Current Research* (pp. 9-18). Newbury Park, CA: Sage.
     ------------ (1989). Intercultural adaptation. In M.K. Asante and W.B. Gudykunst (eds.), *Handbook of International and Intercultural Communication.* (pp.275-294). London: Sage.
     Klapp, O. (1969). *Collective Search for Identity.* NY: Holt, Rinehart, and Winston.
     Kluckhohn, F. R. and F. L. Strodtbeck (1961). *Variations in Value Orientations.* Evanston, IL: Row, Peterson.
     Kochman, T. (1981). *Black and White Styles in Conflict.* Chicago: University of Chicago Press.
     Kovel, J. (1984). *White Racism: A Psychohistory.* NY: Columbia University Press.
     Kroeber, A. and C. Kluckhohn (1952). *Culture: A Critical Review of*

Concepts and Definitions. Cambridge, MA: Harvard University Ethnology Papers.

Kroeber, A. and T. Parsons (1958). The concepts of culture and social system. *American Sociological Review,* 23: 49-61.

Kuhn, T. (1970). *The Structure of Scientific Revolutions.* Chicago: University of Chicago Press.

Ladner, J. (ed.). (1998). *Death of White Sociology.* Los Angeles: Black Classic Press.

Lather, P. (1992). Postmodernism and the human sciences. In S. Kvale (ed.), *Psychology and Postmodernism.* (pp. 88-109). London: Sage.

Levine, L. (1977). *Black Culture and Black Consciousness.* NY: Oxford Press.

Lieberson, S. (1985). Unhyphenated Whites in the United States. In Richard Alba (ed.). *Ethnicity and Race in the U.S.A.: Toward the Twenty-first Century.* (pp.159-180). London: Routledge and Kegan Paul.

Lincoln, Y. and E. Guba (1985). *Naturalistic Inquiry.* Beverly Hills, CA: Sage.

Lindlof, T. (1995). *Qualitative Communication Research Methods* (vol. 3). London: Sage.

Linnaeus, C. (1964). *Systema Naturae 1735.* NY: Coronet Books.

Littlejohn, S. (1992). *Theories of Human Communication.* (4th ed.). Belmont, CA: Wadsworth.

Lovejoy, A. (1960). *The Great Chain of Being.* NY: Harper and Row.

Lyman, S. (1972). *The Black American in Sociological Thought.* (p.94). NY: G.P. Putnam's Sons.

Madhubuti, H. (1992). *Black men: Obsolete, Single, and Dangerous? The Afrikan American Family in Transition.* Chicago: Third World Press.

Marshall, C. and G. Rossman (1989). *Designing Qualitative Research.* (pp. 105-148). London: Sage.

Martin, J., M. Hecht and L. Larkey (1994). Conversational improvement strategies for interethnic communication: African American and European American perspectives. *Communication Monographs,* 61: 236-255.

Mbiti, J. S. (1970). *African Religions and Philosophies.* Garden City, NY: Anchor books.

McCall, G. J. and J. C. Simmons (1978). *Identities and Interaction* (rev. ed.). NY: Free Press.

McCombs, H. (1991). Black self-concept: an individual/collective analysis. *International Journal of Intercultural Relations,* 9: 1-18.

McCracken, G. (1988). *The Long Interview* (Sage University Paper Series on Qualitative Research Methods, Vol. 13). (pp. 16-22). Beverly Hills, CA: Sage.

Mead, G. H. (1909). Social psychology as counterpart to physiological psychology. In A. J. Reck (ed.), *Selected Writings: George Herbert Mead.* Chicago:Chicago University Press.

------------ (1910). Social consciousness and the consciousness of meaning. In A.J. Reck (ed.), *Selected Writings: George Herbert Mead.* Chicago: Chicago University Press.

------------ (1913). The social self. In A.J. Reck (ed.), *Selected Writings: George Herbert Mead.* Chicago: Chicago University Press.

Merton, R. K. and P. Kendall (1946). The focused interview. *American Journal of Sociology,* 51: 541-557.

Merton, R. K., M. Fiske, and P. Kendall, (1956). *The Focused Interview.* Glencoe, IL: Free Press.

Milliones, J. (1980). Construction of a Black consciousness measure: Psycho-therapeutic implications. *Psychotherapy Theory Research and Practice,*

17(2): 458-462.

    Mintz, S. and R. Price (1976). *Birth of African American culture: An Anthropological Perspective.* Boston: Beacon Press.

    Montagu, A. (1945). On the phrase 'ethnic group' in anthropology. *Psychiatry: Journal for the Study of Interpersonal Processes,* 8(1): 27-33.

    ------------ (1962). *Culture and the Evolution of Man.* (p. 38) NY: Oxford University Press.

    ------------ (1974). *Man's Most Dangerous Myth: The Fallacy of Race.* NY: Oxford University Press.

    Montgomery, D., M. Fine, and L. James-Myers (1990). The development and validation of an instrument to assess an optimal afrocentric world view. *The Journal of Black Psychology,* 17: 37-54.

    Morgan, D. (1988). *Focus Groups as Qualitative Research.* (Sage University Paper Series on Qualitative Research Methods, Vol. 16). Beverly Hills, CA:Sage.

    Myers, L .J. (1988). *An Afrocentric World View: Introduction to an Optimal Psychology.* Dubuque, IA: Kendall-Hunt.

    ------------ (1991). Expanding the psychology of knowledge optimally: The importance of world view revisited. In Reginald L. Jones (ed.), *Black Psychology.* (pp. 15-32) Berkeley, CA: Cobb and Henry Publishers.

    Myrdal, G. (1944). *An American Dilemma: The Negro Problem and Modern Democracy* (2 vols.). NY: Harper and Row.

    Namenwirth, M. (1986). Science through a feminist prism. In R. Blair (ed.), *Feminist Approaches to Science.* (pp. 18-41). NY: Pergamon Press.

    Nichols, E. (1976). *The Psychological Aspects of Cultural Differences.* Ibadan, Nigeria: World Psychiatric Association.

    Nicotera, A. M. (1993). Beyond two dimensions: A grounded theory model of conflict-handling behavior. *Management Communication Quarterly.* 6(3): 282-306.

    Nobles, W. (1986). Ancient Egyptian thought and the development of an African (Black) psychology. *Kemet and the African World View.* In Maulana Karenga and Jacob Carruthers (eds.), Los Angeles: University of Sankore Press.

    ------------ (1991). African philosophy: Foundations of Black psychology. In R. L. Jones (ed.), *Black Psychology.* (pp.47-64). Berkeley, CA: Cobb and Henry.

    Oberg, K. (1960). Culture shock: Adjustment to new cultural environments. *Practical Anthropology,* 7: 170-179.

    Ogbonnaya, A. O. (1994). Person as community: An African understanding of the person as an intrapsychic community. *Journal of Black Psychology,* 20: 75-87.

    Omi, M. and H. Winant (1986). *Racial Formation in the United States: From the 1960s to the 1980s.* NY: Routledge and Kegan Paul.

    Pajaczkowska, C. and L. Young (1992). Racism, presentation, psychoanalysis. In J. Donald and Ali Rattansi (eds.), *'Race,' Culture and Difference.* London: Sage.

    Parenti, M. (1969). Ethnic politics and persistence of ethnic identification. In H. Bailey and E. Katz (eds.), *Ethnic Group Politics.* Columbus, OH.: Charles E. Merrill.

    Parham, T. (1989). Cycles of psychological nigrescence. *The Counseling Psychologist,* 17(2): 187-226.

    Park, R. (1950). *Race and Culture.* NY: Free Press.

    Philipsen, G. (1987). The prospect for cultural communication. In D. L. Kincaid (ed.), *Communication Theory: Eastern and Western Perspectives* (pp. 245-254). NY: Academic Press.

    Rampersad, A. (1976). *The Art and Imagination of W.E.B. Du Bois.* NY:Schocken Books.

Rattansi, A. (1992). Changing the subject? Racism, culture, and education. In J. Donald and A. Rattansi (eds.), *'Race,' Culture and Difference.* London: Sage.

Reinharz, S. (1983). Feminist research methodology groups: Origins, forms, functions. In V. Peraka and L. Tilly (eds.), *Feminist Revisions: What Has Been and might be.* (pp. 197-228). Ann Arbor: University of Michigan Press.

Rich, A. (1974). *Interracial Communication.* NY: Harper and Row.

Robinson, P.W. (1978). *Black Quest for Identity.* Minneapolis, MN: Burgess Publishing.

Rubin, R. and Martin, M. (1994). Development of a measure of interpersonal communication competence. *Communication Research Reports,* 11(1): 33-44.

Ryan, J. (1973). *White Ethnics: Their Life in Working Class America.* New Jersey: Prentice Hall.

Ryle, G. (1949). *The Concept of Mind.* NY: Hutchinson Publishing.

Sachdev, L., R. Bourhis, S. W. Phang, and J. D'Eye (1987). Language attitudes and vitality perceptions: Intergenerational effects amongst Chinese Canadian communities. *Journal of Language and Social Psychology,* 6: 287-307.

Samaj, L. (1981). The Black self: Identity and models for a psychology of Black liberation. *Western Journal of Black Studies,* 5(3): 158-171.

Sarbin, T. and J. Kitsuse (1994). A Prologue to Constructing *the Social.* In T. Sarbin and J. Kitsuse (eds.), *Constructing the Social.* (pp. 1-18), London: Sage.

Schutz, A. (1967). *The Phenomenology of the Social World.* Evanston, IL.: Northwestern University Press.

Scotton, C. M. (1988). Self-enhancing codeswitching as interactional power. *Language and Communication,* 8(3/4): 199-211.

Shimanoff, S. (1980). *Communication Rules: Theory and Research.* (p.57). Beverly Hills, CA: Sage.

Silberman, C.E. (1964). *Crisis in Black and White.* (p. 73). Clinton, Massachusetts: Colonial.

Singer, M. (1987). *Intercultural Communication: A Perceptual Approach.* Englewood Cliffs, NJ: Prentice-Hall.

Slugoski, B. R. and G. P. Ginsburg (1989). Ego identity and explanatory speech. In J.Shotter and K.J. Gergen (eds.), *Texts of Identity.* Newbury Park, CA: Sage.

Smith, M. J. (1988). *Contemporary Communication Research Methods.* Belmont, CA: Wadsworth.

Sowell, T. (1975). *Race and Economics.* NY: David McKay.

Staples, R. (1973). What is Black sociology?: Toward a sociology of Black liberation. In J. A. Ladner (ed.) *Death of White Sociology.* (pp. 161-172) NY: Random House.

------------ (1987). *The Urban Plantation: Racism and Colonialism in the Post Civil Rights Era,* (pp. 51-74). Oakland, CA: Black Scholar Press.

Starosta, W. J. (1974). Quantitative content analysis: A Burkeian perspective. In W.B. Gudykunst and Y.Y. Kim (eds.). *Methods for Communication Research* (185-194). Beverly Hills: Sage.

Stebbins, R. (1992). *Sociology: The Study of Society.* NY: Harper and Row.

Stoddard, L. (1920). *The Rising Tide of Colour.* NY: Charles Scribner's Sons.

Strauss, A. (1978). *Negotiations: Varieties, Contexts, Processes, and Social Order.* San Francisco, CA: Jossey-Bass.

Tajfel, H. (1981). *Human Categories and Social Groups.* Cambridge: Cambridge University Press.

------------ (ed.). (1982). *Social Identity and Intergroup Relations.*

Cambridge: Cambridge University Press.

Templeton, J. (1994). *The focus group: A Strategic Guide to Organizing, Conducting, and Analyzing the Focus Group Interview.* Chicago: Probus Publishing Co.

Terrell, F. and S. L. Terrell (1981). An inventory to measure cultural mistrust among Blacks. *Western Journal of Black Studies* 5(3): 180-184.

Thomas, C. W. , ed. (1971). *Boys No More: A Black Psychologist's View of Community.* Beverly Hills, CA: Glencoe Press.

Ting-Toomey, S. (1986). Interpersonal ties in intergroup communication. In W.B. Gudykunst (ed.), *Intergroup Communication.* (114-126). Baltimore, MD.: Edward Arnold.

------------ (1989). Identity and interpersonal bonding. In M.K. Asante and W.B. Gudykunst (eds.), *Handbook of International and Intercultural Communication.* (pp. 351-373). London: Sage.

Turner, R. (1962). Role-taking: Process vs. conformity. In A. Rose (ed.), *Human Behavior and Social Processes.* (pp. 20-40). Boston: Houghton Mifflin.

------------ (1968). The self-conception in social interaction. In C. Gordon and K.J. Gergen (eds.), *The Self in Social Interaction,* 1: 93-106. NY: John Wiley.

Tylor, E. (1871/1889). *Primitive Culture: Research into the Development of Mythology, Philosophy, Religion, Language, Art, and Custom.* NY: Holt.

Walker, C. (1991). *Deromanticizing Black History: Critical Essays and Reappraisals.* Knoxville: University of Tennessee Press.

Watzlawick, P., J. Beavin, and D. Jackson (1967). *Pragmatics of Human Communication: A Study of Interactional Patterns, Pathologies, and Paradoxes.* NY: Norton.

Weber, M. (1961). The ethnic group. In Talcott Parsons (ed.) *Theories of Society* 1: 305. Glencoe, Ill: The Free Press.

Webster, Y. (1992). *The Racialization of America.* NY: St. Martin's Press.

Weimann, J. M. (1977). Explication and test of a model of communication competence. *Human Communication Research,* 3: 195-213.

Welsing, F. (1991). *The Isis Papers:The Keys to the Colors.* Chicago: Third World Press.

West, C. (1993/1994). *Race Matters.* NY: Vintage Books.

------------ (1993). *Prophetic Fragments.* Trenton, NJ: Africa World Press.

White, J. L. (1991). *Toward a Black Psychology.* (pp. 5-14). Berkeley, CA: Cobb and Henry.

White, J. L. and T. A. Parham (1990). *The Psychology of Blacks: An Afro-American Perspective.* Englewood Cliffs, NJ: Prentice Hall.

Wilson, A. (1978). *The Developmental Psychology of the Black Child.* NY: Africana Research Publications.

------------ (1990). *Black-on-Black violence: The Psychodynamics of Black Self-annihilation in Service of White Domination.* NY: Afrikan World Infosystems.

------------- (1993). *The Falsification of Afrikan Consciousness: Eurocentric History, Psychiatry and the Politics of White Supremacy.* NY: Afrikan World Infosystems.

Woodson, C. G. (1933). *The Mis-education of the Negro.* Washington, D.C.: The Associated Publishers.

Woolf, H. (ed.). (1977). *Webster's New Collegiate Dictionary* (6th ed.). Springfield, MA: G. and C. Merriam Company.

X, Cedric, D. P. McGee, W. Nobles, and N. Akbar (1975). Voodoo or IQ: An introduction to African psychology. *The Journal of Black Psychology, 1,* 61-78.

Author Index

Subject Index

About the Author

RONALD L. JACKSON II is Assistant Professor of Speech & Communication
Theory at Pennsylvania State University in University Park, Pennsylvania.

ISBN 0-275-96184-2

EAN

9 780275 961848

HARDCOVER BAR CODE